M-34
252

W9-BVG-604

The Art of Illustrating Sermons

THE
ART
OF
ILLUSTRATING
SERMONS

Ian Macpherson

ABINGDON PRESS

New York   •   Nashville

THE ART OF ILLUSTRATING SERMONS

Copyright © 1964 by Abingdon Press

All rights in this book are reserved.
No part of the book may be reproduced in any manner whatsoever without written permission of the
publishers except brief quotations embodied in critical articles or reviews. For information address
Abingdon Press, Nashville, Tennessee.

Library of Congress Catalog Card Number: 64-15759

SET UP, PRINTED, AND BOUND BY THE
PARTHENON PRESS, AT NASHVILLE,
TENNESSEE, UNITED STATES OF AMERICA

to Margaret my wife
in gratitude for twenty-five years together

Preface

Not every author can honestly claim that before putting pen to paper he studied all the books on his subject. In the present case the claim is not as big and boastful as it sounds, for the plain fact is that on this branch of homiletics the literature is amazingly meager—a bare half-dozen slim volumes.

In order of the dates of their publication they are as follows: *Lectures to My Students* (Fourth Series), by Charles Haddon Spurgeon; *The Art of Sermon Illustration*, by Harry Jeffs; *The Art of Illustrating Illustrated*, by John Edwards; *The Art of Illustrating Sermons*, by Dawson C. Bryan; *The Craft of Sermon Illustration* (now incorporated with the larger volume *The Craft of Sermon Construction*), by W. E. Sangster; and *Let There Be Light*, by Benjamin P. Browne.

All these I have read with profit, and to each I am more or

less indebted. In addition, I have gone carefully through the relevant sections of over three hundred books on preaching in general, and I have gleaned much of very great value from their pages.

Detailed acknowledgments are made in the text, and for every assistance afforded me I am most grateful.

IAN MACPHERSON

Contents

1

Looking Them Over

In her captivating study of that colorful and controversial
figure, Salvador Dali—one of the few great living artists—Fleur
Cowles tells of a curious mistake he once made. Having under-
taken to write his biography, she appealed to him by letter for
"a one-page account of himself." In reply he sent her a roughly
drawn and fantastically misspelled catalog of his accomplishments, describing himself as mystic, philosopher, architect,
jeweler, novelist, and so on. Glancing down the column, she
suddenly realized that he had left out the one thing which, above
all others, he is divinely designed to be. He had said nothing
about painting! And later, when she pointed this out to him
and rallied him about it, "he smilingly added a line to the long
list—and then, at the bottom of the page: *et aussie peintre!*"
And also painter!

Are not we preachers sometimes prone to a similar error?
Asked to specify the personal qualities prerequisite to success
in our holy calling, we would probably refer readily enough to
warm spirituality, profound scholarship, a pleasing presence,
sociability, a good carrying voice, and the rest—all of which are,
of course, matters of more or less moment. The likelihood is,
however, that many of us would say nothing whatever about a
further factor which, although obviously secondary in one sense,
is nevertheless primary in another—facility in the art and craft
of illustration. We have forgotten about painting!

11

Some ministers, to be sure, have gone to the opposite extreme. Impressed with the importance of the illustrative element in preaching, they have accorded it excessive and unwarranted prominence, cultivating it at the expense of the message itself. Such men as "Ian Maclaren," Joseph Hocking, and Lloyd Douglas, either took up storytelling as a romantic sideline to the Christian ministry, or else abandoned their professions altogether to devote themselves to novel writing. To do so is a pity. Far better is it to keep one's storytelling within the framework of the preaching office.

"I want to know a butcher paints," wrote Robert Browning in his poem "Shop." Well, doubtless it is desirable that on occasion the man behind the counter should become the man before the canvas. He may be all the finer tradesman for being something of an artist. But with us preachers it is different. Where we are concerned, some measure of artistry is no mere holiday hobby, no optional occupation of the leisure hour—it is an integral and inalienable part of our total task. Only, our painting is not with pigments on boards; it is with words on the living canvas of human minds and hearts.

But what is an illustration? Confronted with this inquiry, one is strongly tempted to copy the evasive circumlocution of Shakespeare's Bardolph, who, being required to give the meaning of "accommodated," hedges thus, fumbling after a definition: "Accommodated; that is, when a man is, as they say, accommodated; or when a man is, being, whereby a' may be thought to be accommodated." Evidently the slippery fellow felt that the wisest way to explain the difficult verb was in terms of its usage, to show what it signified by indicating how it was employed. So with sermon illustrations. In seeking to set forth what they are, the best line to take is to try to define them according to function.

What, then, are the functions of sermon illustrations? Surprising though it may be to those who are disposed to disparage and depreciate them, we can, without incurring the charges of exaggeration and redundancy, point to no fewer than seventeen purposes which they can serve in sermons. Let us review them in rapid succession.

To begin with their most obvious function, illustrations can help us to make our meaning plain. Clarity is a first essential in preaching, and word-paintings are of high value because they can assist us to be clear. Not always do printers' "devils" appear as angels of light; but compositors sometimes do, as witness the well-known case of the man who, when setting up the type for a new edition of the Bible, got one letter delightfully wrong in I Cor. 13:1: "Though I speak with the tongues of men and of angels, and have not clarity, I am become as sounding brass or a tinkling cymbal."

Two considerations press upon us as preachers the duty of being as plain as we can. One is the fact that the message we are bidden to deliver is in some ways abstruse and profound, and the other is that we normally address a popular audience.

It goes without saying that if we are to present the truth to others with what Quiller-Couch called "heavenly clarity," we shall have to be clear about it ourselves. How is this to be secured? Gordon W. Ireson recommends in this connection a capital custom of his own.

I have myself made it a systematic practice for years to supply my own illustrations when reading a theological book. Suppose I were trying to teach this truth to others: how would I illustrate it? What is the point or principle involved? What is analogous to it in everyday experience? It has been an exacting but immensely profitable discipline. If I can't produce an illustration, it is because I haven't properly understood the point at issue.[1]

Was it not Lord Kelvin who declared that he was never certain that he had fully grasped an idea in engineering until he could make a model of it? Illustrations are the models which ensure

[1] *How Shall They Hear?* (London: S.P.C.K., 1957), p. 99.

that when discussing profound realities in the pulpit we know what we are talking about.

Obviously, however, our principal purpose in illustrating is not to clarify the deep things of God for ourselves but to try to do so for others. That is our major problem. As Samuel Mc-Comb dryly remarks: "Unhappily there are in every congregation persons who are not intelligent, or at least not intelligent when they cross the threshold of a church!" But we must not be too hard on them. Two reflections ought to modify and to mollify any disappointment with them we may feel in this direction.

The first is that whatever the average intelligence level of our listeners and however educated and cultured they may be in other fields, they have not had, where theology is concerned, the benefit of specialized technical training that we have had; and, speaking generally, they are not accustomed, as we are, to tough, consecutive thinking. Behind the following observation by Henry Ward Beecher there is the wisdom of experience. "There are few men," he contends, "who can follow a close argument from beginning to end; and those who can are trained to it, though of course some minds are more apt for it than others." To much the same effect is this more recent remark by R. E. C. Browne: "Most people, even educated people, do not listen analytically, but are affected by the pattern of imagery in an utterance."

The second tempering reflection is no less impressive. Not only have our hearers not had the training requisite to easy and full comprehension of our message, but neither have they had the time during the previous week that we have had to pay special heed to the topic on which we propose to speak. That matter is the subject of a monitory note by Thomas M. Morrow. "We need always to remember," he writes, "that whereas we have spent days in preparing our sermon, so that it has become part and parcel of our being, the congregation has to take in its message in some twenty to thirty minutes. A truth which is crystal clear to us, because we have pondered long over it, may not be nearly so clear to them, however carefully it is explained." In our preaching we ought to strive after perspicuity because of the intellectual limitations of our listeners. Always our aim should be not merely to put things so plainly that it will be possible for the dullest in our congregation to understand us, but so to put things that it will be impossible for him to misunderstand us.

Even more cogent and compelling is the second consideration which lays heavily upon us the duty of lucidity—the fact that the message we are called upon to deliver is in some senses deep and dark and difficult. It is indeed a simple gospel, but it is a gospel by no means reserved for the simple. In it there are depths which the profoundest intellect cannot plumb; depths in which, as James Denney said, "We can hear the plunge of the lead into fathomless waters." To grapple with such great and glorious realities is a task far beyond our finite human reason, much less vividly to communicate them to our congregations. If we are to present them intelligibly we shall have to interpret the spiritual by the natural, the unknown by the known, the abstract by the concrete, the general by the particular. In other words, we shall have to illustrate. Often an illustration is the spark that bridges the gap between truth and the mind, a spark that flashes out so brilliantly that what is seen can never be forgotten. It has been well said that an idea which cannot be painted is an idea which ought not to be presented to a popular audience. God's ideas are paintable. They can be transmitted in pictorial form, and often that is the only form in which they can be transmitted.

Consider two homiletic transparencies which illuminate subtleties of thought otherwise perhaps impenetrably opaque to ordinary minds.

Suppose that sometime we want to elucidate for our people the distinction between an ideal and a standard. In relation to Christ the distinction is, we feel, a crucial one, and we are determined that our hearers shall feel that too. How are we to set about drawing out the distinction? We may do so by sketching a word-picture, and this is the sort of word-picture it will have to be:

Imagine a man who is a tailor by trade, but who is also an artist in his spare time. As a tailor, he is expected to adopt certain standards. His yardstick and measuring tape are required to conform to the official regulations. As an artist, he has an ideal. Visiting the famous galleries of Europe, he feasts his eyes on the old masters. Raphael, Michelangelo, Tintoretto, with all their wizardry and enchantment, fire his imagination and challenge him to copy and compete with them. Now, between the standard to which, as a tailor, he is commanded to conform and the ideal to which, as an artist, he aspires, there is a certain surface resemblance. Both exert a powerful influence over him, and both lay a claim upon him. But, despite the seeming similarity, there is between them a deep and radical difference. That difference is this: Nobody blames the tailor when his poor daubs utterly fail to reproduce the magic of the masters; if, however, his instruments of measurement do not meet legal requirements, he may be sent to prison.

You see the point? To be a poor painter is a misfortune rather than a fault; to be a bad tailor is to be guilty of a breach of the moral code. The one is pardonable, the other punishable. The former betokens artistic limitation; the latter, deliberate infringement of civil law. Now, Jesus is not just an ideal to which we may aspire, and which we may approximate if we so desire; he is the divinely appointed standard with reference to which we are all now being tested, and in accordance with which we shall all at last be acquitted or condemned.

The other transparency attempts to illustrate a principle on which the Christian may proceed in his acceptance of the authority of Christ in regard to questions for the present beyond the bounds of ordinary human knowledge and experience. Here it is:

When I was a lad at school in Scotland, we had in one of our classrooms a large pasteboard globe, mounted on a metal pedestal, on which was printed in bright colors a map of the world. Now and then, in meditative mood, I would slowly spin the globe round with the tips of my fingers. On it I could see the names of places then strange to me—Tokyo and Toronto, Iceland and New Zealand. And, as I looked at these names, I wondered at times whether, where they were concerned, the cartographer could be relied upon. Black dots, small or large, and brilliantly painted areas represented on his map towns, cities, and countries which, for aught I knew to the contrary, might have had no existence outside of his own imagination. How was I to know that they were not mere figments of his fancy? I'll tell you what I did with that map maker. I checked up on him within the region where I could put him to the proof. I looked on the globe for a place called Edinburgh, and I found it. I looked for a place called Glasgow, and I found it. I looked for a place called Aberdeen, and I found it. Thus to my own satisfaction I established the fact that the cartographer was correct insofar as I was then able to verify his reckonings. And afterward I went on to make what I felt was a warrantable deduction from the evidence. I argued like this: "If the map maker is right, and if I have discovered that he *is* right within the range of my present experience, surely I may justly presume that he is right also with reference to spheres beyond my present experience. Meantime I will take his word for it, trust him where I cannot trace him, and someday I shall find that he was absolutely true in regard to *all* the places marked on his map."

It is like that between my soul and Christ. Some of the things Jesus tells me, I cannot for the present verify. Concerning them, I must at the moment take him at his word. But these are not the only things he says. There are other things of which he speaks, moral and spiritual things, and about these I have put him to the test; and, having found him true in relation to them, I trust him in connection with other matters now beyond the reach of my inquiry and investigation.

illustrations

Passing to the second function which illustrations can perform, we observe that they promote persuasion. The fact that persuasion is necessary implies that there is in the human heart not only inability to see what God has revealed, but likewise at

17

times unwillingness to accept it. Apt word-pictures can do more than clarify a clouded and complicated issue; they can compel assent to an unpalatable fact. They can persuade. To be sure, it is always perilous to try to prove a point by telling a tale, but a tale which embodies eternal truth is almost morally irresistible.

In support of that contention here are two graphic examples.

A proposition to the rightness of which certain people may find it hard to agree without some sort of pictorial persuasion is that, imperative and urgent as it is in these revolutionary times for us to proclaim the social implications of the gospel, by far the most impressive contribution most of us can make to the moral betterment of the world is to be ourselves committed and witnessing Christians. The following illustration places that point beyond the possibility of honest cavil:

Picture an old man living in a cottage in a little village. His cottage was once whitewashed, but is now dirty and in sore need of exterior decoration. Now suppose that someone comes up to that old man and points out to him that his house is in shocking condition and that steps ought immediately to be taken to improve its appearance. The old man agrees, but explains that he is too poor to be able to pay for the cost of the materials. The other man promises to provide them if the old man will himself do the job. It is a bargain, and in due course the cottager is supplied with what he needs to carry out the undertaking. But that old man, we will assume, has a social conscience. Before applying the whitewash, he takes a walk through the village. As he does so, he sees that his is not by any means the only house requiring decorative attention. There must be more than a dozen of them in a like condition. So the old man asks himself what can be done about it. He decides that it will be best to water down the whitewash until there is enough to go round. What happens? Not one cottage in the village is one whit the whiter for the application of the practically colorless fluid. If anything, they all look worse than before.

Another proposition we may find it hard to get our hearers to accept without pictorial persuasion is that Jesus expected to be taken seriously when he said that one soul is worth more than the whole world. "What is a man profited if he shall gain the whole world, and lose his own soul?" (Matt. 16:26.) Many are disposed to dismiss that utterance as romantic, religious hyperbole. Our Lord, they remind us, was an Oriental; and Orientals, they declare, use exaggeration for emphasis, so that all Jesus intended to do by that saying was to heighten to some degree in his listeners' minds the sense of human values. For ourselves, we may have no hesitation in believing that he meant quite literally what he said, but we should have the utmost difficulty in bringing others round to our way of thinking on the matter by a mere process of reasoning. An illustration can enable us triumphantly to carry our point. This, for instance:

Suppose that somewhere in these parts during the past week a young married woman has given birth to her first baby. And suppose that, as she lies there in the hospital with her nursling in her arms and the rapture of new motherhood on her face, I go up to her, and I say: "How much do you want for the child?" She shows no inclination to do business with me, so I proceed to offer her inducements. I offer her London, but she hugs the little mortal to her heart and refuses to sell him at that price. I offer her Great Britain, but still she declines to conclude a bargain. I offer her Europe, but she continues deaf to my proposal. At last I offer her the whole world; but now she presses the tiny bundle of humanity more tightly than ever to her breast, as she replies—and, mark you, she is not just *saying* it, she really *means* it: "My baby is worth more to me than all the world!" If she doesn't say that, she is no true mother; and so, when we adopt love's outlook on human beings, we endorse Christ's estimate of human values.

Illustrations

The third function fulfilled by illustrations is that they cause <u>our discourses to come alive.</u> "How does it happen," asks Gene E. Bartlett, in sheer bewilderment, "that so often we take the Word of Life and make it lifeless?" That is indeed an inexplicable mystery, yet the fact is that at times we do. "Dull as a sermon" is a phrase which has passed into a proverb, and the

19

tragedy is that all too frequently the proverb is not without justification.

To be sure, we preachers may point out in self-defense that the gospel is old, that what is old leaves people cold, and that it is only novelty which has the power nowadays to attract attention. But that is no valid excuse. The antiquity of the gospel no more robs it of freshness than the fact that the sun shone a thousand years ago this morning impairs today the pristine glory of its light. And, in any case, even if the gospel were in need of vitalization, that is a service which can be rendered by a vivid and arresting illustration. "It is because the preacher has an oft-told tale to set before his people," wrote Andrew Fuller, "that the subject-matter of Christian teaching pre-eminently requires illustration." Graphic and gripping word-pictures can make our message live.

Here is how. Our theme, we will assume, is that of Easter, and our object is to electrify our congregation with the conviction that Christ has triumphed over the tomb, that he is there and then omnipotently alive, and that his presence in the church that day is of infinitely greater consequence for our worship than even the veracity of the Holy Volume or the beauty of the sacred building. Is there any more impressive manner in which we could bring this to bear on their minds than by means of some such word-painting as this?

Picture an old lady living in London about the middle of last century. Her hero, we will suppose, is the Duke of Wellington, and when we first see her she is sitting in her drawing room, a copy of his biography open in her hands. She is reading the account of the Battle of Waterloo, and as she reflects on the role the duke played in that famous engagement, and on all that the victory he then won has meant for her as an Englishwoman, she is overwhelmed with gratitude and devotion to him. Every now and again she lifts her eyes from the page and looks up at an etching hanging on a wall of the apartment. It is a pen-and-ink drawing of Apsley House, Wellington's London residence; and, as she gazes at it, she says to herself:

"How wonderful to think that the great duke lives there!" Then, all at once, her reverie is broken into by a sharp rap on the door. She rises to respond to it and, when the door is opened, there confronting her in living presence is the duke himself! In a flash book and building—fascinating though they are—are alike forgotten, for the conqueror meets her face to face!

Something far more marvelous than that frequently happens in a Christian church. People go there to listen to the reading and exposition of a Book, which tells of a triumph immeasurably surpassing Waterloo, or to gaze with rapture on the stately fabric of some glorious cathedral. And, all at once, there comes a knock on the door of their hearts. There before them is none other than the risen Christ himself!

illustration

But, again, to name yet another of the functions of illustrations, we may note that they can adorn our addresses. By adding beauty to the presentation of the message, they can increase its popular appeal. Some preachers would, of course, warmly debate the propriety of employing illustrations ornamentally, and no doubt this sort of thing can be overdone. A. E. Cowley, for instance, contends that "even if they have little or no relevance to the theme, anecdotes or references to local and current affairs give picturesque interest to an address." That, surely, is carrying things too far. Closer to the mark is J. H. Jowett's contrast of the decorative table lamp, which draws all eyes to itself, and the streetlamp, which, itself unseen, sheds light on the dark road. Yet even streetlamps need not be without a charm of their own, combining beauty with utility, adorning while they enlighten. "An illustration," observes Henry Ward Beecher, "is never a mere ornament, although its being ornamental is no objection to it." Perhaps the finest thing ever said in this connection is a comment by Horton Davies on the sermons of W. E. Sangster. He says that they are "like Greetings Telegrams, admirably embroidered with imagery which does not detract from the urgency of his communication of the good news."

21

There is, however, a peril to be avoided when employing imagery in preaching. It is a peril to which both preacher and listener are exposed—that of stopping at the image instead of looking past the image to the thing symbolized and the truth taught. When the preacher stops at the image, he becomes a mere storyteller, content if he can entertain the congregation with his tales. When the hearer stops at the image, an appeal may be made to his aesthetic sensibilities, but no lasting mark is made upon his thinking and character. About this danger John A. Kern issued in his day a word of warning. "Just as the abuse of images in worship," he declared, "is to stop at the image and adore that—worship through images degenerating into image-worship—so the chief danger in the case of illustrations is that the hearer may stop at the illustration and not pass by means of it to the truth itself."

Nevertheless, despite this possible peril most of us will probably want to go on giving our sermons, insofar as we can, touches of what Phillips Brooks called "splendour," by introducing into them on occasion a decorative illustration.

Still a further function illustrations can fulfill in our sermons is to spice them with variety. Variety is vital to the effective delivery of a discourse. "A sermon without variety," wrote A. T. S. James, "is as disheartening as a road without a bend." However high the standard of our preaching, if it consists of nothing but argumentation and exhortation, it can become extremely tedious. The listener longs for diversity. In his *Lives of the Poets*, Samuel Johnson justly remarks: "The great source of pleasure is variety. Uniformity must tire at last, though it be uniformity of excellence." Of course, there are other legitimate modes of diversifying our preaching. We can do it by regularly ringing the changes on all the available themes; we can do it by altering from time to time our type of treatment; we can do it by introducing variations into our postures, our gestures, and into the pitch and pace and volume of our voices. Undoubtedly, however, the most successful way of lending variety to our sermons, without deflecting the minds of the listeners from the theme under survey, is to insert at strategic points in the discourse apt, graphic, dramatic illustrations.

Yet another function which illustrations can fulfill is that they help to keep the sermon as short as possible. Brevity, according to the adage, is the soul of wit; it is certainly something which must ever characterize the preacher who would have the wit to save souls. Many sermons, especially evangelistic sermons, lose lamentably in force by being too long. People brought during the earlier part of the discourse to the brink of decision draw back and continue uncommitted because the address is unduly extended. How, then, is brevity to be attained? Illustrations enable us to be short without omitting anything necessary to the adequate presentation of the truth. They make for concision, compression, condensation. "I use the metaphorical," explained George Meredith, "to avoid the long-winded." In preaching, as we shall see later on, there are times when it is imperative, if the delivery is to be impressive, that a simile be lengthened or a tale spun out in the telling. Usually, however, illustrations have the opposite effect. As Thomas M. Morrow maintains: "An illustration can reveal the meaning of a truth in a few seconds, but an explanation might take several minutes." On the whole, illustration means abbreviation.

In addition to all this there is yet another benefit which illustrations can bring to preaching: they can facilitate rhetorical repetition. As preachers we are often placed under the necessity of repeating ourselves, not because we are short of something fresh to say, but because, unless we do, many in our congregation may miss our meaning. Only by judicious reiteration can we, to borrow Richard Baxter's striking expression, "screw the truth into men's minds." To be sure, there will be much in our sermons which requires no repetition. "Only a fool would repeat everything," observes Andrew Blackwood. But he adds: "Only a dunce would see nothing worth repeating." Nevertheless, it is not only the worth of the utterance, it is the dullness of at least

23

some in the audience which makes reiteration obligatory. There is an instructive and impressive story—told, I seem to remember, of one of the United States presidents—which relates how once he took his son with him on an electioneering campaign. In every speech he made during the tour, the seasoned political orator kept saying the same things over and over again, until at last the lad began to think that his father had run out of ideas. With a son's frankness, he said so. "No, my boy," corrected the father. "You see, the first time I make a statement, one fifth of my listeners grasp my meaning. Next time I make it, one quarter understand. The third time, one half. The fourth time, three quarters. And by the time I have made it on five occasions everybody has got it." The tale is probably apocryphal, but there is point in it all the same. There are, of course, exceptions; but where most congregations are concerned, rhetorical repetition in the pulpit is essential to complete comprehension in the pew. Yet if we are to repeat ourselves without wearying our hearers, we shall have to repeat ourselves without *seeming* to do so, and the best way to do that is to use illustrations, reiterating in figure what we have previously proclaimed as fact.

Another manner in which illustrations can minister to the effectiveness of our preaching may now be mentioned. With his genius for *le mot juste*, W. E. Sangster says that they can "earth" a sermon. Some sermons definitely need earthing. Of Samuel Taylor Coleridge, William Hazlitt discerningly and aptly commented that "he had wings but wanted hands and feet." That criticism would apply to much of our preaching. Our sermons are far too speculative and theoretical, leaving the hearers, as it were, hanging in midair. And our sermons are like that because we ourselves tend, by the very nature of the sort of life we lead, to become persons like that. On this subject R. F. Horton has some wise and weighty words:

Abstract modes of thought grow upon us too easily when we spend much time with books and in the reverie of study. Illustrations

24

become tiresome and impertinent to a trained thinker. The fascination of close and connected reasoning and of convincing the understanding by logical methods becomes ever more irresistible to a growing mind. To breathe in the higher circles of thought and to see the small matters of the field or market-place from a serene altitude is undoubtedly proper to a philosopher; and, if a preacher studies diligently and exercises himself in the company of great thinkers, he is apt to become a philosopher and insensibly to drift away from common life and lose touch with ordinary people.[2]

The picturization of one's message saves one from developing this mentality. To be good sermon illustrators we must be keen students of men and things, keeping our eyes wide open, and ever watching in life itself for word-pictures by means of which to picture the Word. Naturally, if we have our heads habitually in the clouds, we should not be surprised if we acquire misty minds; but, if we maintain a lively interest in our fellows and in the world around us, we shall find much of illustrative value which will help us in our discourses to anchor high doctrine to the doing of homely tasks. Illustrations can keep us tethered to common things.

The next end illustrations can serve in discourses need not detain us long: they can assist us to preserve a proper balance in the divisions. To recommend the use of pen-paintings as mere literary "padding" in preaching may well seem a very profitless procedure. Discourses stuffed with materials merely for the sake of size or symmetry are likely to be too artificial to be effective vehicles of eternal truth. Still, as every tailor knows, padding has its points. It makes for good proportions, shapeliness, and beauty of form and structure. In the composition of the sermon, situations arise in which, having said all we can say by way of direct statement under some particular heading, we still have not said sufficient to bring that division up to the same dimensions as the corresponding divisions of the discourse. When that hap-

[2] *The Word of God* (London: T. Fisher Unwin, 1898), pp. 284-85.

pens it is, I judge, perfectly in order to introduce relevant pictorial matter in the interests of balance and proportion. Commenting on the ministry of F. B. Meyer, David Williamson observes that "he never told a story merely because he wanted to expand his address, but always with the definite intention of impressing a thought." Yet surely both objects can be achieved at once.

A further mechanical service which illustrations can render in our sermons is that they can make our transitions smooth. Acting as bridges between the paragraphs, they can enable our hearers to pass easily and comfortably from one division to another. Such "juncturae," as they are technically termed, like the crossings on a railway line, are inclined to give the listeners unpleasant jolts; and in truth if the transitions are not gently negotiated, and if one section of the address does not lead naturally and inevitably into the next, the impression made upon the minds of the members of the congregation may be that the sermon is just a series of disjointed, unrelated paragraphs. Connective word-pictures can eliminate, or at any rate minimize, such jerks and jolts in the progress of our thought and cause the passage from one division to another to be as graciously gradual as that from night to day.

Over and above these functions which illustrations fulfil, there is this likewise to be advanced in their favor: they appeal to all classes of hearers. We preachers have at times the mortification to find that something we say in the pulpit—some finely turned phrase, sparkling epigram, or brilliant flash of inspiration—while delighting a few of our listeners, leaves most of them absolutely cold and unimpressed because they lack the ability to grasp or appreciate it. Thus, while some in our audience smile with pleasure or at least brighten with intelligence when the thing is said or the point made, the others stare up at us with blank incomprehension or downright exasperation. Now, it is neither kind nor wise to make anybody feel inferior in the house of God, where theoretically we are all equal. Illustrations lessen that risk. Understood by all, they are welcomed by all, and put us all on the same level. Even a small child can take in a tale. A good story has the key to every heart.

Near neighbor to this is the next function which illustrations discharge: They establish reciprocity between speaker and listener. This is a prime prerequisite to effective preaching. It should be obvious that we can no more address the people to any real purpose before we are thus en rapport with them, than we can converse on the telephone with a correspondent until he picks up the receiver at the other end of the line. Illustrations break down inhibitions in the audience and set flowing freely the currents of thought and feeling. They focus the attention, fire the imagination, stir the emotions, and, as we say, "take the hearers out of themselves." That is an immense gain. Once our listeners are in that state, we can do what we like with them. A well-chosen word-picture is like the telephone exchange which switches us through.

Closely analogous is still a further function which illustrations fulfill: They "rest" the congregation. "Give the hearer mental breathing-spells now and again," counsels Samuel McComb, and John Broadus goes so far as to say in the same connection that in preaching "an illustration is a psychological necessity." He means, of course, that minds unaccustomed to sustained reasoning at high levels—minds, in fact, like those of the majority of our listeners—require at intervals during the delivery of the sermon periods of rest and relaxation if they are to follow with interest and intelligence the development of our arguments. Of Hugh Latimer it is recorded that in the middle of a sermon he would suddenly break off with the remark: "I will tell you now a pretty story to refresh you withal." Preachers of modern times have also profitably adopted this expedient to expel languor and excite expectancy in their audiences. In a racy volume of random recollections, A. Lindsay Glegg tells that F. B. Meyer once said to him: "Don't be afraid of bringing a little humour into your message. I try to, even if I have to drag in a story,

27

THE ART OF ILLUSTRATING SERMONS

generally about half way through my address. You can't keep your audience tensed up all the time. You must allow them to relax. Remember laughter and tears lie close together." "It is often wise," observes George A. Buttrick, "to allow a congregation to sit down awhile on a milestone and rest. A judiciously placed and chosen illustration will serve that purpose." Doubtless this sort of thing can be carried to extravagant extremes. In that case, as H. G. Hammerton comments, word-pictures sometimes "instead of illustrating a point can become little more than light relief." Nothing can justify that. The preacher's pulpit stories are designed not to entertain but to enlighten. Yet, as they enlighten, they may help to reduce in the congregation the tension of sustained consecutive thinking. How often have we seen our hearers, after straining for awhile to follow some abstruse argument, relax into easy comprehension at the telling of a story!

Illustrations also aid memory. It is no uncommon thing for the only part of a discourse which lingers in the minds of listeners after a lapse of years to be a living word-picture. George Herbert found that to be true in his time. Of "The Parson Preaching" he wrote: "Sometimes he tells them stories, for them also men heed and remember better than exhortations; which, though earnest, often die with the sermon: but stories and sayings they will remember." To the same intent is the following utterance of Thomas Guthrie: "By awakening and gratifying the imagination, the truth makes a deeper impression on the memory. The story, like a float, keeps it from sinking; like a nail, fastens it in the mind; like the feathers of an arrow, makes it strike; and, like the barb, makes it stick."

In addition to the functions of sermon illustrations already listed there is this also that, as Batsell Barrett Baxter admirably expresses it, "they enforce a point by indirection." Philip Doddridge quaintly compares evangelical preaching to "a lancet concealed in a sponge," and never is the lancet so successfully hid-

28

den as when buried deep in the heart of an illustration. In the world around us, and in the lives of those with whom we come into close contact, we, as public servants of God, are bound to observe many things which it is our moral duty to expose and oppose. Making a frontal attack on such evils might defeat its own object by calling forth in those against whom it was directed resentment or retaliation, or at best some measure of self-justification. But a piercing illustration can penetrate all such defenses, as did the prophet Nathan's vivid little vignette penetrate those of King David. Nathan did not in his approach to his sovereign begin with a forthright condemnation of the king's dark double sin. Instead he told a disarming story about a rich man who, he alleged, had robbed a poor man of his one ewe lamb; and then, when David's anger flashed forth at the fictional offender, the prophet pointed in the king's face and cried: "Thou art the man!" As Alexander Whyte powerfully put it: "Nathan's sword was in the king's breast before David even knew that Nathan had a sword!" The lancet was well concealed in the sponge, and the effect was annihilating. "An illustration," says Austin Phelps, "has more authority than a command—the authority of perceived moral reality." A narrative such as Nathan's can sometimes provide, as it were, a smoke screen under cover of which we may reveal and rebuke a rooted wrong; since, as A. T. Cadoux cogently contended, "A parable often hides the truth until it is too late for the hearer to guard himself against it."

One of the foremost functions of sermon illustrations is to touch the heart. Of D. L. Moody, Silas Hocking declared: "Surely never had a man such a stock of stories as he had, and nearly all of them tear-compelling, and surely no man could tell a story better than he." Doubtless in Moody's day that sort of thing was grossly and vulgarly overdone; but may it not be that in our own time when, as someone has aptly said, "men's lachrymal glands have become hypertrophied," we have swung to the opposite extreme and are afraid to tell a tender tale lest we be charged with sentimentality?

That there is a peril in this connection cannot be contested. It is the peril of moving people by a story rather than by the Story, of kindling their imaginations and rousing their emotions without dealing with them in the depths of their beings, of producing a merely psychological rather than a moral and spiritual impression. Martyn Lloyd-Jones warns us against this in the following pertinent paragraph:

I remember hearing a story concerning a preacher who was endeavouring to convince his congregation of the danger of delaying decision and action. As an illustration, he pictured a number of people staying at the seaside, who had walked one afternoon on to a promontory of rock stretching from the beach. They had walked right out on to this rocky point and the sea lay all around them. They were enjoying the view and looking out to sea. They failed to realize that gradually the tide was coming in on both sides of them and that it was about to cut them off at the point where the promontory joined the mainland. There they were—so enjoying the sunshine and the fishing that they were unaware of their peril. Then, suddenly, someone noticed it and the urgent question arose as to whether their retreat was already cut off. Were they already surrounded? Would the sea soon cover the whole promontory? And were they all to be drowned?

The preacher had taken much time in presenting the story, and had done it with such dramatic effect that he brought the congregation to a point when it seemed to be doubtful whether anybody in the party could escape at all. At that point he suddenly shouted: "If you do not run at once, it will be too late!" It is said that literally the whole congregation rose to its feet and the chapel was speedily emptied.[3]

Without question that was a moving narrative, but it did not move the hearers in the right way. Its emotional appeal as a

[3] Conversions: Psychological and Spiritual (London: Inter-varsity Fellowship, 1959), pp. 34-35.

story was so strong that its point was bypassed and its moral missed.

Yet things need not be like that. A well-told tale can touch the heart in such wise as to tell on the life. Here, from the pen of W. R. Maltby, is a poignant word-painting to prove it:

I may be permitted to recall an instance which came within my own knowledge. A good many years ago I knew a workingman in the north of England whose wife, soon after her marriage, drifted into vicious ways, and went rapidly from bad to worse. He came home one Sunday evening to find, as he had found a dozen times before, that she had gone on a new debauch. He knew in what condition she would return, after two or three days of a nameless life. He sat down in the cheerless house to look the truth in the face and to find what he must do. The worst had happened too often to leave him much hope of amendment, and he saw in part what might be in store for him. He made his choice to hold by his wife to the end and to keep a home for her who would not make one for him. Now that a new and terrible meaning had passed into the words "for better, for worse," he reaffirmed his marriage vow. Later, when someone who knew them both intimately, ventured to commiserate him, he answered: "Not a word! She is my wife! I loved her when she was a girl in our village, and I shall love her as long as there is breath in my body." She did not mend, and died in his house after some years, in a shameful condition, with his hands spread over her in pity and in prayer to the last.[4]

Maltby adds: "I hope that no apology is needed for providing a concrete and contemporary instance of what love to the uttermost may really mean." Surely not! What an illustration that episode from real life in the modern world is for a sermon on Hosea! What an illustration for a sermon on an infinitely greater than Hosea!

The crowning function that illustrations can fulfill in sermons is that they can lead to conversion. They can constrain our lis-

---

[4] *Christ and His Cross* (Apex ed. Nashville: Abingdon Press, 1963), pp. 54-55. Used by permission of Epworth Press.

31

teners toward commitment to Christ. If anybody disputes that, its truth can be demonstrated by this touching personal testament of C. E. Allen:

Some sixty years ago, being on holiday in a small village on the River Severn, I attended the Sunday-school Anniversary service at the local Nonconformist chapel. It was not for the desire to worship that I did so, but purely for the fun of hearing the "country bumpkin" children sing. There was a local preacher conducting the service, and I was not at all impressed in the first part of the sermon; though, strangely enough for such a type of service, he had chosen for his text the agonized cry of Christ upon the Cross: "My God, My God, why hast Thou forsaken Me?" But suddenly something he said, I know not what now, brought me wide awake, just in time to hear him tell the following story, by which he sought to explain the meaning of the words of the text. It concerned a motherless little girl, who had been left in the sole care of her father. As the years went by, they became all in all to each other. Then the little girl became ill with a poisoned foot, and a consultation between a local doctor and a surgeon took place, to see what was best to be done regarding it. The decision they came to was that the child had no chance of recovery unless part of her leg was amputated. Their question then was how, and by whom, was the child to be told. And the doctors decided that the father was the best and only one to do it. At length, with great reluctance he accepted the extremely painful task. How he got through that ordeal he could never afterwards tell. And it was made all the more awful by the strange request the child made. After an intensely painful silence, she said: "Daddy, I will have it done if you will make me one promise." "And what is that?" asked the anxious father. "If you will promise to put your arms around me, and look straight into my eyes," she replied, "then I will consent." Who can tell the agony of the father's heart as he pondered over that terrible request? Yet, rather than lose his beloved child, he knew it must be done, as brokenly he made answer: "My darling, I promise." The day came when the operation was to take place, and the father carried out his promise. But as the surgeon proceeded with his grim task (for this was in the days before painless operations were performed), and the father saw the growing anguish in his

32

child's face, he could bear it no more, and was forced to turn his face away. Immediately, the cry rose from the heart of the child: "Father, Father, you promised to look at me," and with that cry on her lips she fainted dead away.

It is not needful for me to describe how the preacher applied the story to explain the meaning of the soul-anguished cry of Jesus Christ. Sufficient is it for me to say—that simple story revealed to me, as in a vision, the wonderful love of God the Father in its redemptive power. Through it my whole life became completely changed, until, from a careless, skeptical, godless youth, I was led to become a preacher of the redeeming love of God in Christ. Never have I regretted the decision then taken, though sixty years of many and varied experiences have passed away. It was the one unregrettable step I ever took." [5]

There, then, are the seventeen functions of illustrations. Faced with such an imposing array of possibilities, how can any sensible and fair-minded preacher question the wisdom of making wide but discriminating use of them in sermons?

Yet many do. Five excuses which such preachers tender for excluding them from their preaching may here be summarily specified.

The first is that of those who maintain that the modern sermon is so brief that in it there is simply no room for illustrations.

What are we to say to that? Well, it is patent that in our time sermons have been ruthlessly shortened. We are a long way now from Henry Parry Liddon's eighty minutes. Alexander Whyte's half that speaking span, "forty minutes with a leaning to mercy," is frowned upon as over long. Even John Ruskin's "thirty minutes to raise the dead in" is regarded as excessive. A quarter of an hour or twenty minutes is, we are told, all we may warrantably expect from a modern audience.

And, to be sure, if this demand for sermonic brevity is legitimate, and if it is to be yielded to, we shall very likely be placed

[5] *Christian World.*

33

under the necessity of pruning from our preaching all pictorial materials. Illustrations are almost certain to be excised as dispensable extras.

But is this demand for brief sermons defensible and is it to be acceded to? Up to a point, yes. Beyond all question, the old "three-decker" type of discourse which Lloyd George graphically compared to a cumbersome man-of-war, "needing an hour's sea-room to turn in," was much too long. Yet the plea for short measure in the ministry of the Word of God—almost, one would think, the only connection in which people seem to want short measure—must not be permitted to be pressed too far. Arbitrarily to set limits to the length of the sermon is unwise, because factors enter into the situation which call for a certain measure of elasticity. There is, for instance, the preacher himself. What sort of person is he? One man can be more tedious in ten minutes than another in sixty. Then there is the nature of the topic under treatment. Some subjects can be adequately dealt with in half an hour, others are too vast to be thus quickly dismissed. Of one thing we may be sure: If a sermon is too short to be illustrated, it is too short to be preached.

The second objection to the employment of illustrations in preaching is that the whole sermon ought itself to be an illustration. That was James Denney's contention. He himself never used word-pictures, and he sought to defend his refusal to do so on the ground that what is really wanted is not illustration but lucidity. It is deeply interesting, all the same, to note that however his conscious mind may have protested against the practice of putting illustrations in sermons, his unconscious mind was keenly aware of the need for them. This may be inferred from the remark he once made that sometimes, when proclaiming the fact of the Cross, he was tempted to envy the Roman Catholic priest the crucifix which, while preaching, he holds in his hand, and to which he can simply point and say: "God loves like that!" Surely for such a purpose a literary image in the sermon would be infinitely more impressive than an ivory

34

image on an ebony rood? Unknown to himself, Denney was seeking something more than the limpid lucidity which he praised so highly in preaching and which was the chief merit of his own style. He was seeking illustration.

The third objection to the use of word-paintings in sermons is that illustrations are an insult to the intelligence of an adult congregation. No doubt some illustrations are. We recall Ronald A. Ward's relishless recipe for a certain type of modern sermon: "Take a few pretty stories, mix well with some moral platitudes, place in the refrigerator, and serve cold." Such "pretty stories" are more fit for the nursery or kindergarten than for the church. Yet it would be crazy to include all stories in the same category, and A. Lindsay Glegg thinks that failure to realize this is responsible for the comparative disregard of this vital branch of homiletics in many divinity schools. "Our theological colleges have, I think," he says, "almost entirely neglected this most effective aid to preaching, the idea being apparently that 'stories,' 'anecdotes,' may be all right for children, but quite out of place in a respectable sermon." That is an erroneous notion. It is no exaggeration to claim that most of the popular preachers, at any rate, do not consider it beneath their dignity to illuminate their message and that their most cultured listeners love to have it so.

The fourth excuse for not using illustrations is put forward by those who, rightly or wrongly, protest that as preachers they lack the happy knack of doing so successfully. Some men, they insist, are born storytellers, combining the gifts of the reporter with those of the raconteur, and possessing a natural aptitude for self-expression through the medium of dramatic narrative. Modestly, these others disclaim such powers, maintaining that while for those who have them pictorial preaching may be all very well, for such as they themselves it can never be anything more than an impossible dream.

Even eminent ministers of Christ have confessed to that feeling—R. W. Dale, for instance. He said frankly that it wasn't in him. "An illustration," he declared, "is my despair."

35

What are we to say in reply? Well, we must, of course, candidly concede that there are vast differences in natural endowment. Some men certainly are born storytellers. In *Memory-Hold-the-Door*, John Buchan says of himself: "I suppose I was a natural storyteller, the kind of man who for the sake of his yarns would in prehistoric days have been given a seat by the fire and a special chunk of mammoth. I was always telling myself stories when I had nothing else to do—or, rather, being told stories, for they seemed to work themselves out independently." We are not all John Buchans, and yet we may share to a greater degree than we suspect his gift of narration. In any case, let us in this regard remind ourselves of Henry Ward Beecher's cautionary and comforting words: "Many of you will find it [sermon illustrating] natural to you. But do not be discouraged, even if it *is* natural, that you do not at once succeed. Why should you succeed before you learn the rudiments of your art? You are educable."

The fifth reason adduced by certain ministers for their refusal to illustrate their sermons lies in an ill-founded fear lest their message somehow suffer thereby. John Wesley seems to have been half ashamed of his illustrations. He pruned them ruthlessly from his sermons before publication. Billy Graham, at least in his earlier days, went even further, including no pictorial materials of any kind in his addresses. His aim was to storm the wills of his hearers rather than to stimulate their imaginations. Yet, if I may make a personal confession, of all I have read of what he has written it is a striking word-picture which stands out most boldly in my recollection. Here is the illustration:

The story is told (I believe it to be a true one) of a young man who was working under the hood of his Model T Ford, trying in vain to make it run. After a long time, in which he had had no success, a fine automobile stopped beside him. A well-dressed man stepped out, went over to the young man and, sensing his difficulty,

36

told the would-be mechanic to make a certain minor adjustment in the timing of the motor. Rather reluctantly, the young man did so. "Now," said the man, "your car will run." With a turn of the crank, the motor started running like that of a new car. Surprised that such a man should know about machinery, the young man said: "But how is it that you know just what to do to my car to make it run? Who are you?" Quietly the other said: "I'm Henry Ford. I made the car. I know all about its workings." [6]

That is a capital way of illustrating the wisdom of taking our personal problems for solution to our Maker. Certainly, Dr. Graham could have made the point by other means; but it is more than doubtful whether he would have made it so effectively. Despite the hesitations and misgivings of these notable evangelists, we may safely conclude that no pulpit discourse ever suffered by suitable illustrative presentation.

But enough on the negative side. Let us, in closing this chapter, pass again to the positive, clinching with three crowning considerations our contention that sermons should be aptly and amply illustrated.

The first is that the gospel is itself a story. Of this we are reminded when we trace the term to its Anglo-Saxon root— "godspel," "good story." "Christianity," wrote D. M. Baillie, "is a story; and, as I like to put it, it is a story with a plot." Luther called the Evangel "gute mar," "good tale." Not always does the etymology of a word provide a clue to its correct interpretation; it does here. For what, after all, is the gospel but a good story, God's story? "The storyteller," it has been said, "creates a world with words." God is the great Storyteller, for by his Word he created countless worlds. From us men, however, the finest story he has to tell is the story of his love revealed in Jesus Christ. And that is the story we are commissioned to relate. As J. H. Jowett has expressed it: "A preacher is a

[6] *Best Sermons 1955*, ed. G. Paul Butler (New York: McGraw-Hill Publishing Co., 1955), p. 297. Used by permission of G. Paul Butler.

man with a story to tell, and there has never been pressed into human language a story so matchless in its fulness and so marvellous in its power as the story of Jesus."

It cannot too strongly be stressed that the Christian religion is not primarily a system of philosophy, a set of dogmas, or a code of ethics. It is first and foremost a story; not a story spun by man on the web of his own fancy to account for the phenomena of nature and of human life—as are, for example, the classical Greek myths—but a story of something that actually happened in history, a story which is the divine key to the understanding of the universe and the mystery of being.

But how does one win popular acceptance for a story? There are two lines one may take to begin with. The first is to tell the story itself, and the second is to recount other stories which confirm it.

We must tell the story itself. Only a fool would contend for the credibility of a narrative without first relating it. How are people to know whether or not a tale is true until they hear what it is? A story is not, in the prime instance, for argument; it is for announcement. It is not for discussion; it is for narration. It must be related before it can be debated. That is frequently overlooked in connection with the communication of the gospel.

The second line we may take in gaining credence for our story is to tell other stories which confirm it. Obviously, a narrative capable of substantiation by relevant analogies is likelier to be true than one which does not admit of such pictorial endorsement. Illustrations are vital in preaching because they supply such analogical corroboration. Listeners will more readily believe in spiritual realities when they see them brilliantly reflected in the scenes, situations, incidents, and persons of the natural order.

That, then, is one consideration constraining us to include word-paintings in our pulpit work. The gospel is itself a story, and to be put over successfully a story must first be related and then corroborated by other stories.

The next consideration urging us to illustrate our sermons is that we live in a picture age. Stories have, of course, cast a powerful spell over the minds of men in every generation, but in the present era this human love of the pictorial has become far more prevalent than ever before. Ours is par excellence the Age of Illustration, an age when people are habituated to picture-thinking. Now, we preachers cannot afford to ignore the prevailing tone and temper of our time. We are not to deliver our message in a social vacuum; we are to proclaim it on the stage of contemporary history and against the background of current events. This is the Age of Illustration, and it will certainly be good policy for us to approach it by way of illustrations. In truth it is hard to see how otherwise we can address it with any reasonable hope of impressing it at all.

"How is it possible to pierce the mentality of an age that is film-fed, radio-glutted and jazz-intoxicated," demands Robert Menzies, "unless we master the art of vivid presentation and succeed in turning the ear into the eye?" How indeed? In this regard the prodigious popularity of the modern novel ought to give us preachers pause. Entering a public library and looking around, we see standing on lonely shelves the weighty works on history, politics, economics, philosophy, and what have you. But about the stacks containing romances the eager readers crowd like seagulls round a fishing smack coming in with its catch. Remembering that, as Bernard Shaw put it, "no man is a hypocrite in his pleasures," we conclude from what we observe that stories are what people want today, stories with pictures in them. And, if we are wise, we will learn our lesson.

Donald A. Miller tells of a former college president who wrote: "A good moving picture has far more influence than a good sermon." That we doubt; but if it has, it is because there have been no moving pictures in the sermon. "It is sometimes said in a tone of reproach," comments Carl S. Patton, "that most people think in pictures. So they do. So far as we think about things that can be put into pictures, we always think in pictures whenever we think distinctly." To match this pictorial interest in the modern congregation, the minister must preach pictorially. That is the second consideration.

The third and last is that this was the Master's method. Such is the supreme warrant and incentive of the illustrative preacher. Jesus preached pictorially. The rhetorical question with which he began so many of his parables, "Whereunto shall I liken the Kingdom of Heaven?" was not an appeal for illustrative assistance; it was simply a formula for winning his hearers' closest heed, for he himself well knew where to find the exact, inevitable analogy. What a wide range of realities and activities was pressed into pictorial service in his teaching! The objects of nature and the pursuits of men were alike conscripted. As Tyrrell Green lyrically phrases it:

> He spoke of lilies, vines and corn,
> The sparrow and the raven;
> And words so natural, yet so wise
> Were on men's hearts engraven.
>
> And yeast and bread, and flax and cloth,
> And eggs and fish and candles—
> See how the most familiar world
> He most divinely handles.

A. M. Hunter says that the parabolic element in Luke's Gospel amounts to 52 per cent of the total. Thus more than half of one of the evangelical memoirs is pictorial in form, and of the whole of the recorded teaching of our Lord the ratio is much higher—something like 75 per cent. Surely a most impressive proportion.

Nor, if it is not bordering on the blasphemous to say so, was

Jesus an illustrative preacher because by the peculiar bent of his mind he was prevented from being an effective argumentative preacher. On the contrary, the New Testament contains not a few examples of his superb dialectic skill. Consider, for instance, his crushing rejoinder to the Pharisees when they criticized him for healing a man on the Sabbath. Pointing out that to comply with the requirements of the Mosaic law they themselves administered the rite of circumcision—a wounding of the human body—on that day, he demanded with ineluctable cogency why he should be taken to task not for maiming but for mending a man on the Sabbath! Or consider his consummate handling of the complicated case of the woman taken in adultery. Caught red-handed in the act, what doubt could there be that she was guilty? Yet the tender heart of Jesus would not let him be accessory to the infliction of the penalty. He was on the horns of a dilemma. On the one hand, he wanted to uphold the law; on the other, to free the woman. How could both be done? Jesus knew. Stooping down, he wrote on the ground and said something which altered the whole situation. "He that is without sin among you, let him first cast a stone." Or, once more, consider how cleverly he extricated himself from the verbal trap baited for him by the Herodians with their tricky question about taxation. Calling for a coin, he held it up in full view of the congregation and inquired: "Whose image and superscription is written thereon?" Instantly, they rejoined: "Caesar's!" "Well, then," said Jesus, "give Caesar what belongs to him." In debate Christ was deadly. Always he had the last word, and always he closed the discussion in a manner that made his interlocutors gasp. When he had had his say, there was nothing more to be said. We are not surprised to learn from Luke that a time came when "they durst not ask him any question at all" (Luke 20:40).

In view of this, is it not highly significant that the Master deliberately and of set purpose adopted in preaching the pictorial technique? "It is impossible to believe," wrote John Oman, "that the conveying of His message through illustration, through picture, and in relation to the world of nature and of men, was not a considered method to which He gave much thought." If that is true—and who will deny that it is— ought we not as preachers in this as in every other direction to labor to be like our Lord?

There is a story of how once in a famous European art gallery a young artist stood for awhile in front of a magnificent masterpiece. The geometric accuracy of the perspective in the painting, the power and movement of the drawing, the delicate blending of the gorgeous colors, moved him to the depths of his being. Tears welled up in his eyes. Someone, noticing this, asked him what was the matter. Pointing to the picture, the youth exclaimed: "I can't paint like that! I never shall be able to paint like that!" Then for a moment he lapsed into silence. Presently, however, his face brightened. He saw things from a new angle. "Thank God," he cried, "I am a painter too!"

Studying the stories of Jesus, with their exquisite literary form and extraordinary moral force, we ministers of the Word resemble that young man. We know that we cannot paint word-pictures like these. We know that we shall never be able to paint word-pictures like these. But, thank God, we are pictorial preachers too!

2

Sorting Them Out

The process of sorting things out is one with which we are all familiar. Instances of it abound on every hand. We find it, for example, at the post office, where numbers of people are constantly employed, classifying the contents of the "mixed bag" which comes in from the mailboxes, and allocating the mail to the various towns, countries, and continents to which it is assigned. We find it, again, at the coast when the trawlers arrive with their catch, the fish being carefully graded alike as to species and as to individual quality, and packed in barrels and baskets accordingly. We find it, once more, at the bank when the cash is presented at the counter—a miscellany of loose change and paper money—and there is swiftly reduced to order by the teller, who divides it into its different denominations, placing the coins each in its proper pile, and laying the notes on top of one another in their appropriate bundles.

Something analogous there must be where illustrations are concerned. They, too, need sorting out. Just as there are different types of art—richly tinted oil paintings, vivid, jet black silhouettes, sharp-edged etchings, and so on—so various kinds of word-pictures may be used in sermons.

To classify is to clarify. So let us sift out illustrations, sorting them into the types into which they may be divided, and supplying specimens of each.

Note, first, that *single words* can illustrate. "How frequently,"

43

exclaims Spurgeon, "a word is itself a picture!" In point of fact, of course, as the science of semantics intimates, every letter of the alphabet was originally a picture or symbol of some thing or thought. Writing of the ancient Egyptians, R. G. Ikin says:

They used pictures of flowers, birds, and so on, to represent words and syllables. The picture of a disc stood for the sun; then from pictures they passed to symbols, and the disc of the sun came to suggest day by association of ideas. This system of writing was called "hieroglyphics"—that is, "sacred letters" used by the priests for inscriptions on monuments. Ordinary people used these letters in more and more shortened forms; an alphabet gradually grew up; and it was from this simpler form of writing that the Phoenicians later made the alphabet from which we derive our own ABC.[1]

Thus, in a sense, whether we wish to or not, we are bound to preach pictorially. Speech being what it is, we are compelled in the composition of our discourses to employ figure and fancy; forced to use the imagery of language even if we decline to use the language of imagery.

It is, of course, with the latter that we are here principally concerned—the illustrative properties of individual words, their almost magical faculty of conjuring up a scene or "summoning the blood." To be effective preachers we must learn the art of utilizing graphic, picturesque, evocative expressions. For in a sermon single words can flash like rubies.

Advertising agents and others whose business it is to influence public opinion on a large scale are fully alive to the mystic potency which resides in words, sensitively aware of the subtle suggestiveness of the terms they employ and of the emotional response these terms are likely to call forth in those to whom they are addressed. Nothing is left to chance in the choice of

[1] A Pageant of World History (London: Thomas Nelson & Sons, 1928), p. 25.

their catchwords and slogans. Days, perhaps even weeks, may be spent on the selection of a single term.

Take an example. Here, let us say, are two trains, bound from Birmingham to London. One is an express, the other is a slow train. That is, in fact, what the latter is—a *slow* train. But the advertising department of the British Transport Commission will not call it a "slow" train. They will call it a "stopping" train—as if anybody would ever board a train if he feared it would not stop! They will call it a "local." They will even call it "semifast." But they will not call it "slow," because that would beget in the minds of intending passengers undesired reactions. "Stopping," "local," and "semifast" are euphemisms for "slow." They mean the same thing, but they put it rather differently. The advertising agents know what they are about. They recognize the value and importance of individual words.

Obviously, however, it is to the works of professional writers that we must turn if we want to see at its finest this delicate sensitiveness to the subtle nuances of words and the selection of terms exactly fitted to convey the intended impression.

Consider the following instances. E. M. Forster wrote: "I am, or rather have been, a novelist, but in my old age I have *ratted* in the direction of biography." Mark that vivid, vital, vigorous verb. Once I heard W. E. Sangster tell how at a fashionable garden party a bulbous but "dainty" female *ballooned* toward him. Could any other word have so perfectly wedded his purpose? Describing how his famous fictitious manservant, Jeeves, ushered a guest into a crowded room, P. G. Wodehouse said that he *shoveled* him into the apartment; and at once every reader could see the action being performed.

In illustrating our sermons we should, as I say, use live, luminous words. Economical of space and time, there can be compressed into them a wealth of meaning and allusion which otherwise it might take a phrase or even a whole sentence to communicate. That is one significant factor in their favor.

45

Their chief merit, however, is that, like steel, they strike sparks from the flint of people's minds, causing truths which else might have passed unnoticed to blaze into visibility. Hence, while shunning anything in the nature of the bizarre or exotic in our choice of language, and reminding ourselves of A. G. Gardiner's wise aphorism that "a use of fine words is not necessarily the same as a fine use of words," we would do well in our preaching to employ pithy, piquant, picturesque terms.

To see how superbly that can be done, look at this incomparable illustration by Leslie Weatherhead. In it the individual words are hand set, like gems in pure gold. Reading it closely, we cannot but be impressed with the fact that again and again the preacher with fine fastidiousness picks from his extensive vocabulary the exact term he needs, a term for which no precise synonym can be found. Here is the word-picture:

I remember one night in the Mediterranean we passed quite close to Stromboli, the famous island volcano which rises sheer out of the sea. It was after dinner and almost dark. Suddenly there was a great burst of flame from the crater at the summit. Huge tongues of flame shot up hundreds of feet into the sky, lighting up the ocean for miles around. Tons of molten rock were thrown into the air. Through our glasses it was possible to distinguish redhot boulders racing down the mountainside, and gradually a stream of lava forced its way almost to the sea. For many hours—when our vessel had slipped westwards toward the last lingering light of sunset which lay upon the horizon, when the bold outline of Stromboli was lost in the gathering shadows of night—that redhot stream of lava, like some awful open wound, gashed the darkness. What did it mean? It meant that for a few hours there had been revealed those great fires which had been burning in the mountain's heart since the foundation of the world.

I sometimes think about the cross,
And shut my eyes, and try to see

The cruel nails, the crown of thorns,
And Jesus, crucified for me.

But even could I see him die,
I could but see a little part
Of that great love which, like a fire,
Is always burning in His heart.[2]

That, past all doubt, is superb word-painting. Coupled with the quotation to which it is so happily married, and with which it closes and reaches its climax, it serves its author's purpose as well as any illustration could. Notice how Dr. Weatherhead chooses his words with nice care, handling them as if they were jewels, and placing them in just those settings in which their iridescent beauty adds most to the effect produced by the pen-picture as a whole. If we think of some of the terms he uses and try to better them, we shall find that it cannot be done. Such expressions as "tongues," "burst," "racing," "slipped," "awful," "open," "wound," and "gashed," glow like fixed stars. Neither can we improve upon them nor with advantage alter their positions in the structure of the paragraph. About them and their placing there is the inevitability of great art. Tinkering with them or transposing them, we spoil the total impression.

But to go on. Note, next, that phrases can illustrate. Whether the phrase be a familiar idiom, a simple or extended metaphor or simile, it can be employed in preaching to illuminate religious reality.

Let us glance in turn at each of these phraseological forms.

First, idiom. Idiom has been defined as "a phrase or mode of expression peculiar to our own language, and not found in any other." Etymologically, that is true; but if the definition is to be brought up to date it will have to be widened to embrace other forms of speech. Although not exclusive to any one tongue,

[2] The Transforming Friendship (New York: The Abingdon Press, [1929?]).

these figures are characterized by that homeliness and adjectival daring which are the hallmarks of idiomatic expression; "a dry remark," "a thirsty land," "the howling wilderness," "the hungry sea," "the falling night," and the like. Ideas transmitted in these popular tropes are far stronger and more striking when thus expressed than they would be in literal prose. To employ idiom in our sermons will certainly serve to heighten and enhance their effectiveness.

Or take metaphors and similes. These figures of speech are condensed parables. They present truth pictorially in tabloid form. To do their work properly and to avoid absurdity, metaphors must not be mixed. Example: "He had shaken hands with all the crowned heads in Europe." They must, moreover, be at the same time both like and unlike the things they are designed to illustrate; like them, so that the comparisons may be seen to be just, and unlike them, so that there may be no confusion between fact and figure. Example: "At last we unearthed the gardener."

How marvelously and memorably fluorescent in a discourse a well-turned, neatly worded figure can be! Years after they have heard it the listeners will distinctly recall it when every other part of the utterance has long since vanished into oblivion. Here are a few sparkling instances which have stuck in my own memory: Richard Baxter's "mute as fishes," Norman Macleod's "the snoring breeze," and George H. Morrison's "a quenched yesterday."

And now a word about rather more elaborate and extended metaphors. Someone has spoken of "the packed energy of the metaphor," and the description is most apt, for the metaphor is indeed a very dynamic figure of speech. Francis Thompson maintained that a metaphor is usually superior in expressive force to a simile and confessed that when faced with the choice between them he always picked the metaphor. Certainly he minted one of the loveliest metaphors in the language when he spoke of the poppy as "a yawn of fire."

48

Indubitably, the poet was right about the superior "punch" of the metaphor. Simile has always a "like" or an "as" in it, and the "like" and the "as" appreciably weaken it. We can see that at once if we put it to a practical test. Suppose Jesus had said: "I am *like* a door." How greatly that would have diminished the force of the figure! He did not. He said: "I *am* the door." The simile would have been slightly ludicrous; the metaphor is suggestively luminous.

It is superfluous to say that the Bible positively swarms with metaphors. Here are a few: "Israel is a half-baked bannock" (Hos. 7:8)—a Scots translation that, by Sir George Adam Smith; "generation of vipers" (Luke 3:7); "that fox" (Luke 13:32); "thou whited wall" (Acts 23:3), and so forth.

And, of course, outside of the Bible, in the writings of Christian authors, there are thousands of such apt, vivid, and vigorous phrases. Take, for example, Joseph Parker's powerful depictment of sin—"the clenched fist, the uplifted hand, the blow in the face of the Almighty." Or take F. B. Meyer's magnificent description of the love of God for the individual soul—"the Amazon River flowing down to water one daisy." Or, again, take G. H. Morrison's awesome personification of "the last enemy"—"Death, with his uplifted hand, stopping the traffic of this mysterious thoroughfare of time." Or, finally, take W. W. Weeks's inspired portrayal of the biblical character Isaac—"a harmless hyphen between his father and his son." Such metaphors, when we use them in sermons, burst into flame like a struck match.

Or turn to similes. With them, too, the Word of God abounds. Consider these specimens: "as the flame setteth the mountains on fire" (Ps. 83:14); "like a sweeping rain which leaveth no food" (Prov. 28:3); "like a rolling thing before the whirlwind" (Isa. 17:13); "as the horse rusheth into the battle" (Jer. 8:6); "as a cart pressed that is full of sheaves" (Amos 2:13); "like an hearth of fire among the wood, and like a torch of fire in a sheaf" (Zech. 12:6).

49

THE ART OF ILLUSTRATING SERMONS

In preaching, similes are most attractive and illuminative. Many of us find ourselves in hearty agreement with the old lady who said to Thomas Guthrie: "What I like about the Bible is its 'likes' "—adding that she liked them in sermons too. It was the absence of them that roused Robert Hall, the famous Baptist preacher, to criticize in these trenchant and unmeasured terms the pulpit style of one of his contemporaries: "You have no 'likes' in your sermons. Christ told us that the kingdom of heaven was 'like' leaven, 'like' a grain of mustard seed. You tell us what things *are*: you never tell us what they are *like*."

That charge cannot honestly be preferred against most of the world's popular preachers. Almost to a man they were masters of the simile, as the following series of citations shows. Spurgeon speaks of eternity past, "when this great universe lay in the mind of God like unborn forests in the acorn's cup." Henry Ward Beecher, a supreme artist in figurative speech, shall supply three samples. "A man without restraint," he says, "is like a barrel without hoops, and tumbles to pieces." Picturing the lost soul's quest for fellowship with the divine, he has this unspeakably poignant figure—"like a mother feeling at midnight for the child whom death has taken." Of the final fate of the sinner, he declares that it is "like a man falling over a lofty cliff—we see him fall, but do not hear the crash below." With reference to Paul, Alexander Maclaren remarks: "The apostle's mind acquires force by motion, and like the chariot wheel *catches fire as it revolves*." Portraying the face of an old saved profligate, J. H. Jowett declares that it is "like a half-ruined chapel, lit up for evening service"; and of the comfort God sends to a soul in sorrow he says that it is "like birdsong in a thunderstorm." Depending solely on our own efforts to produce and promote religious revival, contends Arthur T. Pierson, is "like propelling a boat by puffing with our own breath at the sails."

Adroitly handled, simile and metaphor can add sparkle and splendor to our pulpit work. They impart color, movement, life to a discourse. Like words printed in gold on a page of black letterpress, they brighten and beautify a minister's message.

Once more, we may note that *sentences* likewise can illustrate. Just as an artist may, in a lightning sketch, with a bare line or two suggest a whole scene, so a skillful and imaginative preacher can make a single sentence glow in a sermon like a brilliant painting on a blank wall. Think, for instance, of this from a "literary" sermon, one of the *Letters* of Samuel Rutherford: "When I am in the cellar of affliction, I reach out my hand for the King's wine." Or this by Robert South: "A blind man sitting in the chimney-corner is pardonable enough; but sitting at the helm, he is intolerable." Or, again, this from Charles Haddon Spurgeon: "God gets His best soldiers from the highlands of affliction." Or this from Cynddylan Jones: "You might as well try to cross the Atlantic in a paper boat as to get to heaven by your own good works." Sentences which thus combine the brevity of the proverb with the beauty of the metaphor immeasurably add to the pungency and potency of the sermon.

Examples or paradigms—which, more often than not, are merely strings of such striking sentences—are one of the most impressive aids in elucidating and enforcing truth. Showing how principles, good and bad, work out or how they apply in different directions, paradigms beget in the hearers' minds alike insight into them and appreciation of them.

Examining a sequence of examples, we note how, as one picture after another is flashed on the mental screen—all diverse and yet all bearing immediately on the one theme—the reality they are designed to illuminate stands forth clearly visible in its various aspects. When a photographer wants to give a true impression of a piece of statuary, he does not take just one shot of it, depicting it merely two-dimensionally; he snaps it from several angles and tries to show as many sides of it as he can. So with examples in preaching. Photographing the text or topic, as it were, from various points of view reveals the truth in its different facets and relations. In preaching, the statement

51

of a principle should be followed by at least one paradigm. If we cannot find an example, the probability is that it is not a principle.

Suppose that sometime we have taken as text for a sermon Josh. 1:2, "Moses my servant is dead; now therefore arise," and that the title we intend to affix to our discourse is "Filling a Big Man's Shoes"—a topic very suitable, by the way, for an address to be delivered at the induction of a young minister to a charge made vacant by the death or retirement of an old and successful pastor. Our plan is first to refer to the difficulty in which a man who occupies this position finds himself, and then most hearteningly to indicate how such a person may, like Joshua, fall back on the divine promise: "As I was with Moses, so I will be with thee" (Josh. 1:5). Illustrating our point about the difficulty, we draw three swift illuminative parallels thus:

It is never easy to fill a big man's shoes. Richard Cromwell found that out when he tried to take the place of his famous father as Lord Protector of England. Thomas Spurgeon discovered it when called upon to succeed his sire, Charles Haddon Spurgeon, in the pulpit of the Metropolitan Tabernacle, London. Bramwell Booth found it true when thrust into the gap created by the growing blindness of the founder and first general of the Salvation Army, William Booth.

I remember seeing once in a town in the north of England a shoemaker's shop, in the window of which was displayed a giant pair of shoes, almost a yard long, the work of the cobbler himself. Beside the shoes was a card with these words: "Yours for nothing—if you can wear them!"

Life often faces us with challenges like that. Here in our text we see Joshua being challenged in this way.

Or it may be that on another occasion our object is to preach on a catena or series of passages, each of which contains an allusion to one of Paul's "mysteries." The passages are as follows: "Now to him that is of power to stablish you according to my gospel, and the preaching of Jesus Christ, according to the revelation of the mystery, which was kept secret since the world began, but now is made manifest by the scriptures of the prophets, according to the commandment of the everlasting God, made known to all nations for the obedience of faith" (Rom. 16:25, 26). "By revelation he made known unto me the mystery . . . which in other ages was not made known unto the sons of men, as it is now revealed unto his holy apostles and prophets by the Spirit." (Eph. 3:3, 5.) "I am made a minister, according to the dispensation of God which is given to me for you, to fulfil the word of God; even the mystery which hath been hid from ages and from generations, but now is made manifest to his saints: to whom God would make known what is the riches of the glory of this mystery among the Gentiles; which is Christ in you, the hope of glory." (Col. 1:25-27.) Labeling the address "Open Secrets," we might speak of (1) the Open Secret of the Gospel; (2) the Open Secret of the Church; (3) the Open Secret of Christian Personality. To launch the sermon successfully we devise an introduction consisting of three relevant examples. The introduction takes this form:

What a delightful and exciting thing it must be to make a great scientific discovery! Of this history provides several classic instances. One thinks of Archimedes, the most brilliant mathematician of antiquity, who lived in Syracuse in the third century B.C. One day in his bath he was pondering the problem of how to determine the specific gravity of bodies, when the solution suddenly dawned on him. So thrilled was he that he ran through the streets of the city in unconscious nudity, shouting: "Eureka! Eureka! I have found it! I have found it!" One thinks, too, of Thomas Edison, pioneer of electronics, and of how in 1877 he was experimenting in his modest laboratory at Menlo Park, New Jersey, on the mechanical reproduction of the human voice. Before him was a wax cylinder on which a message had been recorded. Edison played it back. As he did so, he was moved to the depths of his being and, as his biographer admits, "a little scared," when for the first time he listened to a phonograph. One thinks, yet again—to come closer to our own day—of how, on

53

October 2, 1925, at St. Leonard's-on-Sea, Sussex, John Logie Baird, after having spent long, lean years in seemingly unproductive research in a garret, dashed madly downstairs and grabbing the first person he met, dragged him up to his room, set him down unceremoniously in front of his lamps and cameras and gave him, unknown to the lad himself, the honor of being the first person ever to appear on television! Yes, it must be an intoxicating experience to make a great scientific discovery.

Yet here is Paul telling us of something more wonderful by far —the rapture of those to whom are vouchsafed direct divine revelations, a rapture not reserved for the few who possess the elusive quality of genius, but available to all who by faith lay claim to it.

On another day the topic of a discourse we have on hand may be "Unappreciated Greatness," and the text our Lord's lament, recorded in Matt. 13:57: "A prophet is not without honour, save in his own country, and in his own house." Musing on the matter, we remember noticing in our travels several glaring instances of this; and gradually in our minds a pictorial paragraph shapes itself thus:

The world has not always the wit to recognize real greatness when it sees it. Some of its finest and foremost figures have suffered the most shameful neglect. Think of Sören Kierkegaard. His was certainly, from the philosophical and theological points of view, the highest literary genius Denmark has produced; yet when I searched for his grave I found it in the heart of a common cemetery in Copenhagen, unmarked by any public monument. Or think of Richard Baxter. No minister of Christ during the Puritan era in England was more prominent than he. In spite of chronic ill health and almost continuous pain, his output of religious writing was phenomenal and his preaching and pastoral work for the good of Kidderminster, the town with which for so long his name was associated, is almost without parallel; nevertheless, when I went there for the first time and asked more than a dozen of the inhabitants for information about him, not one of them had even heard of him. Or think of Thomas Coke, the intrepid pioneer of Methodism in America. No one nobler than he was ever nursed in Brecon. But when I visited the place, looking for traces of him, I discovered that there is at its center a noticeboard on which are inscribed the names of persons, objects, and scenes of interest connected with the locality. The birthplace of Sarah Siddons, the actress, is mentioned, but there is no reference to Thomas Coke.

All of which is a contemporary commentary on Christ's pathetic assertion: "A prophet is not without honour, save in his own country, and in his own house."

Such exemplification is exceedingly effective as a pictorial element in preaching. One evening in France I witnessed an enthralling spectacle—a historical pageant in which the Palace of Versailles was floodlit from various vantage points and in lights of different colors—red and green and blue and gold. Beam after beam played in swift succession on the beautiful building, picking out first this splendid architectural feature of it and then that, until, when the climax was reached, the whole structure was a blaze of glory. That is what examples can do in expounding and applying truth. They can make it shine with a luster that sets it forth in all its facets as no mere statement of it or argument for it ever could.

Still, it must be owned that usually when we think of sermon illustrations it is not to words or phrases or sentences or strings of brief examples that our thoughts turn, but to paragraphs. The paragraph is the standard measurement of the illustration. There are preachers, to be sure, who specialize in story sermons, where the whole discourse is just an extended word-picture, but they are the rare exceptions. Commonly, paragraphs are what we mean when we speak of illustrations.

Such paragraphs fall into various categories—analogies, parables, anecdotes, and so on. Between these illustrative types the lines of demarcation have never been firmly and sharply drawn. Imagined Iron Curtains may divide them, but no actual Berlin Walls. Some analogies are parables, some parables analogies, and both can often be quite properly classified as anecdotes.

55

When introducing examples of each, we will make an attempt at rough and simple definition and supply appropriate word-pictures.

The first of these types of pictorial paragraph is the *analogy*. What is an analogy? For our present purpose it may suffice to say that it is a figure in which a comparison is instituted between some person, fact, or circumstance in the natural order of things to a corresponding person, fact, or circumstance in the spiritual order; but a figure in which no story is told or personification involved.

Some men in the ministry have a special flair for this sort of illustration. Possessed of a Platonic cast of mind, they cannot help seeing resemblances everywhere. With their vivid imaginations, they see parallels where nobody else would even dream of looking for them. If, as preachers, we are naturally gifted in this direction, we have indeed cause for gratitude, for it is the Master himself who is the supreme exemplar of this type of mind.

Here are several examples of the use of analogy in preaching.

It may be that sometime we may be moved to deal in a discourse with John 3:19: "Men loved darkness rather than light, because their deeds were evil." A fitting title for the sermon might be "Spiritual Noctivigants," and in the sphere of zoology we may lay our hand on just the illustration we require.

Hard though it is for us to credit it, there are creatures which actually prefer darkness to light. Zoologists call them "noctivigants," and the tribe is more numerous than we commonly suppose. Moths and spiders, bats and owls, rats and mice are all noctivigants, and so, among larger animals, are cats, panthers, leopards, tigers, and other members of the feline family. You will recall William Blake's tremendous lines, beginning:

> Tiger, tiger, burning bright
> In the forests of the night.

Yes, some creatures definitely love darkness rather than light. Asleep by day, they prowl abroad in the dark.

Biologically speaking, man is not a noctivigant. He does not prefer natural darkness to natural light. Morally and spiritually, however, he is a noctivigant. Behind our text lies the authority of our Lord himself: "Men loved darkness rather than light, because their deeds were evil."

Or take another example. Our minds and hearts have been turning, it may be, to I Cor. 15:56, "The sting of death is sin," as the basis of a gospel message. In search of suitable illustrative material we discover to our delight that we are surrounded on all sides by arresting analogies to our subject. We open the sermon thus:

It is strange that in God's fair world so many creatures have been furnished with stings. There are stings in the vegetable kingdom. Touch the testy nettle and it flashes fire. There are stings in the animal kingdom. Ants, bees, wasps, hornets, gnats, mosquitoes, spiders, snakes—all possess poison-secreting glands.

In the moral kingdom there is a sting too—the sting of sin—and it is of this that I want specially to speak now. The apostle says that sin is the sting of death, but we shall not err if we say that it is also the sting of life!

Or take one more example. We are led, let us suppose, to preach on faith. Our text is Gal. 2:20, "The life which I now live in the flesh I live by faith in the Son of God, who loved me, and gave himself for me," and our design is to illustrate the character and quality of this saving faith, and to show what it is, as far as possible, by analogy. Musing upon different ways of approaching our theme, the introduction gradually shapes itself like this in our thought:

It is astounding what faith one person will sometimes place in another. The faith of a patient in a surgeon, for instance, allowing himself to be anesthetized, rendered completely unconscious, and lying numb beneath the nimble knife, trusting solely to the doctor's skill

57

THE ART OF ILLUSTRATING SERMONS

for the success of the operation and perhaps for life itself. Or the faith of a passenger in a pilot, flying alone with him at night through stormy heavens, relying utterly on the airman's navigational knowledge and his ability to manage his machine and to bring it at last to a safe landing. Or the faith of a diver in former days, donning his cumbersome lead-weighted suit and descending into the sea, depending wholly on the surfaceman to keep supplying him with the oxygen without which death would soon claim him in the deep.

From such a pictorial introduction the transition is easy to the faith of which Paul speaks in this passage—a faith which rests for life and death, for time and eternity, on the reality of the risen Christ!

Turn now to a further type of sermon illustration—the parable. To this I have already referred, and so here need do no more than raise the question as to whether the parable is the sort of word-picture which can be effectively employed in modern preaching. Some would say no, except perhaps in children's addresses. Nor can this present-day recoil from the pulpit use of parables be greatly wondered at or roundly reprobated. The attitude is understandable and even pardonable. For the fact is that in former times some ministers made far too frequent and often incompetent attempts at it and quite put people off the parable as a vehicle of spiritual truth.

Besides, there is this to be said—to compose a parable and to deliver it well is no facile undertaking. Of Balaam, the son of Beor, it is recorded that the Spirit came upon him and he "took up his parable." It is advisable for us to be quite sure that we are in the same inspired state before we venture to do likewise.

All the same, a practice which commended itself so powerfully to the Master ought not by his disciples to be lightly set aside.

Consider how impressively the thing can still be done.

Look, for example, at this exquisite parable by A. E. Whitham, one of the rarest of such illustrations to enrich a contemporary sermon. Pretending to report a visit paid by the preacher to the New Jerusalem, it runs thus:

In my wandering I came upon the museum in that city of our dreams. I went in and an attendant conducted me round. There was some old armour there, much bruised with battle. Many things were conspicuous by their absence. I saw nothing of Alexander's or of Napoleon's. There was no Pope's ring, nor even the inkbottle that Luther is said to have thrown at the devil. I saw a widow's mite and the feather of a little bird. I saw some swaddling clothes, a hammer and three nails and a few thorns. I saw a sponge that had once been dipped in vinegar and a small piece of silver. Whilst I was turning over a small drinking cup which had a very honourable place, I whispered to the attendant: "Have you got a towel and basin among your collection?" "No," he said, "not here: you see, they are in constant use." [3]

I defy the man with the world's worst memory to forget that illustration.

Next, look at this gripping parable from the pen of "Mark Rutherford," William Hale White. Its topic is "Faith," and as a description of that quality, as this author construed and conceived it, could anything be more dramatically and dynamically telling? His biographer, Catherine Macdonald Maclean, has this to say about it:

The story is simple and noble. If he had wrought his conception in stone or in bronze it could not have been more firm or more clear. In the economy and simplicity whereby the greatest effect is achieved, in the strength with which the commonest words are invested, in the perfection of the choice of symbol, in the force with which the writer's conviction is driven into the marrow of the reader this story has hardly any equal. The experience described in it is that of a watchmaker of exquisite skill and accuracy, who, when crossing an estuary at low water one hot afternoon, lay down to rest for a moment

[3] *The Discipline and Culture of the Spiritual Life* (London: Hodder & Stoughton, 1938), p. 40.

THE ART OF ILLUSTRATING SERMONS

on the sand under a rock and fell asleep, to waken to find himself surrounded by the tide. There was no way of escape. He knew that it would be high tide at 8:57 P.M. His watch showed him that the time was 7:30 P.M. He calculated that if his watch were accurate, the tide would continue to rise only for an hour and twenty-seven minutes, and that at the rate it was rising it would not reach his lips. But if his watch had gained even in the least degree there was every likelihood that he would be drowned. He had every reason to trust his watch, but as the water mounted higher and higher he fell a prey to ghastly fears. Until 8:30 the desperate struggle continued between his knowledge that his watch had never been wrong by so much as a minute, and his fear, as he had not taken an observation for some weeks, that it might have gained. All the strength in him was poured into this rigid battle with the passion of fear, until at length there came the moment when his fear was beaten down: "his faith was restored; the flutter of his heart ceased; the adversary spread his wings and was seen no more." The tide was round his neck at 8:50, but he threw back his head a little, confident that the moment of deliverance would soon come. At 8:58 "the slow, upward, unruffled creep had ceased." [4]

There we have an unforgettable parable of faith triumphant over fear, a parable which was a living transcript of the author's own experience.

And now look at a graphic parable by Søren Kierkegaard, the Danish philosopher and theologian whose published works have exercised so dominant an influence on the religious thought of the modern world. The following parable of "The Wild Duck" is a piquant example of his parabolic genius:

A wild duck was winging its way northwards one spring day across Europe. Flying over Denmark, it looked down and saw far beneath it a farm in the barnyard of which a flock of tame ducks were feeding. Impelled by the pangs of hunger, the wild duck swooped down among the tame ducks and shared their grain. It liked the grain very

---

[4] *Mark Rutherford: A Biography of William Hale White* (London: Macdonald, 1948), pp. 398-99.

much and grew to like also its newfound friends and to enjoy the feeling of security which came with living on the farm. So, instead of continuing on its course, it stayed on at the barnyard. It stayed for a day, a week, a month and finally resolved to settle down for the whole summer. In the autumn, however, when the wild ducks came sailing south through the wide sky, they passed over the farm, uttering their haunting cries. The duck that had stayed behind heard them. Something stirred within it, a longing for the heights. It flapped its wings frantically, fluttering about a bit, but finally sank to the ground. For, alas, it had eaten too well in the barnyard. Plump and puffy, it found its wings no longer able to support it. "Oh, well," it thought, "there are compensations. My life here is safe and the food is good." After that, for a while, whenever the wild ducks appeared in the heavens overhead, their mate in the barnyard would become strangely excited, flapping its wings and echoing the call and apparently preparing for flight. But with the passing of the seasons those rapturous reactions and aspirations rapidly diminished. Until at last a day came when the wild ducks could fly directly above it without its paying any heed at all.

That, again, is a superb parable. We may never be able to compose anything like it; but if, with the aid of the Spirit of God, we apply ourselves to the art of parabolic preaching, it may be that some day we shall acquire such proficiency that of us, as of our Master, it may be said that "the common people hear us gladly."

There is still another type of sermon illustration which we may now and then profitably enlist for our homiletic purpose— fable. The Oxford English Dictionary defines fable as "a story, especially a supernatural one, not based on fact . . . a short moral tale especially about animals." As soon as fables are mentioned, all informed minds at once think of Aesop, the Brothers Grimm, Hans Christian Andersen, and Lewis Carroll. Each of these famous fabulists has much to contribute to our stock of homiletic stories.

With Aesop the trouble is that many of his fables are too

61

well known to be of much real worth as sermon illustrations. Such apologues as "The Lion and the Mouse," "The Dog in the Manger," "The Fox and the Grapes," and so on, would, one fears, be too familiar to our hearers to arouse their interest, much less sustain their attention. Everybody has heard or read them so often that, unless we have the wit to give to their interpretation some novel twist or turn, it would probably be wise to leave them alone.

Nevertheless, not all Aesop's fables are public property to the same extent. He has many less shopworn samples, whose moral meaning ought not to be missed, and which can be confidently counted upon to cast a deep spell upon our people and touch them to finer issues. No less a person than Martin Luther professed to prize the fables of Aesop next to the Bible itself. It will amply repay us to give one or two of the celebrated fabulist's lesser-known stories a quick look and see whether in our opinion they are usable in contemporary preaching.

Think, for instance, of the fable of "The Ass and the Little Dog." How better could one stress the wisdom of humility and the sanity of recognizing one's own limitations than by recounting this amusing and instructive tale?

The Ass observed how great a favorite the little Dog was with his master—how much caressed and fondled and fed with good bits at every meal; and for no other reason that he could perceive but skipping and frisking about, wagging his tail and leaping into his master's lap—was resolved to imitate the spaniel and see whether such behaviour would not procure for him similar favours.

Accordingly, the master was no sooner come home from walking about his fields and gardens and seated in his easy chair, than the Ass, who observed him, came gambolling and braying toward him in a very awkward manner. The master could not help laughing aloud at the odd sight. But his jest was soon turned to earnest when he felt the rough salute of the Ass's forefeet which, raising itself on its hind legs, pawed him lovingly with its front hoofs and seemed bent upon leaping into his lap. The master, terrified at this outrageous behaviour, called for his servants, who came in and smote the Ass, and soon convinced it that its attentions were not appreciated and that its place was not that of the more favoured little Dog.

Beyond doubt, however, the most serviceable of Aesop's fables from the homiletic point of view is that of "The Body and Its Members." As an illustration for a sermon on I Cor. 12:27, "Ye are the body of Christ, and members in particular," it could hardly be bettered. Says Aesop:

In former days there was a quarrel among the members of the human body. Each part professed itself indignant at being obliged to work for the stomach, which remained idle and enjoyed the fruits of their labour. They one and all resolved to rebel and grant it supplies no longer, but to let it shift for itself as well as it could. The hands protested that they would not lift a finger to keep it from starving. The mouth wished it might never speak again if it took the least bit of nourishment for the stomach as long as it lived. The teeth refused to chew for it so much as a morsel for the future. The solemn covenant was kept as long as anything of that kind can be kept, which was till each of the rebel members pined away to skin and bone and could hold out no longer. Then they found there was no doing without the stomach and that, as idle and insignificant as it seemed, it contributed as much to the maintenance and welfare of all the other parts as they did to its.

Yes—Aesop at his best is very good. But, if even Homer nods at times, we can hardly expect his less gifted compatriot to be always wide awake. Frankly, there are occasions when Aesop's fables—or those attributed to him—fall pretty flat. But we should not permit ourselves to be put off by such lapses from what is on the whole a very high standard. After all, his apologues must have real value when they have held their own modest place in the world's literature for so long. In trying to compose fables of our own, we shall find a study of his work eminently rewarding.

A more up-to-date source of such illustrations are the writings of C. L. Dodgson, better known by his pen name "Lewis Carroll," *Alice's Adventures in Wonderland* and *Through the Looking Glass*. Harry Emerson Fosdick makes occasional use of them to good effect; and well he may, for they are full of a sort of whimsical wisdom thinly disguised by the seemingly "daft" narrative. Behind the nonsense there is a great deal of sense, as witness the following quotation from the former book—a subtly sardonic comment on the modern craze for "progress" without regard to direction or destination. The illustration forms part of a fragment of recorded conversation between Alice and the Cheshire Cat:

"Cheshire Cat," she began, rather timidly, as she did not at all know whether it would like the name; however, it grinned a little wider. "Come, it's pleased so far," thought Alice, and she went on: "Would you tell me, please, which way I ought to walk from here?" "That depends a good deal on where you want to get to," said the Cat. "I don't much care where," said Alice. "Then it doesn't matter which way you walk," said the Cat. "So long as I can get somewhere," Alice added, as an explanation. "Oh, you're sure to do that," said the Cat, "if only you walk long enough!"

Next on our list of types of sermon illustrations is allegory. What is allegory? Someone has satisfactorily defined it as "a fictitious story which conveys an abstract truth in symbolic language." Of it many of the fathers of the early church were inordinately fond. It was their favorite method of biblical interpretation, and they carried it at times to ludicrous lengths. The school of Alexandria in particular erred in this connection. To its representatives there was hardly a narrative in the Old Testament or in Christian tradition as it had been handed down to them which was not amenable to allegorical treatment. Everything to them was figurative, emblematic, metaphorical. The plain sense of a passage was never the true sense. Not the literal, historical meaning but the allegorical one was that of which they were ever in quest.

64

Even Augustine of Hippo, the greatest of them all, fell into this snare of overallegorization. Here is an example of the excessive extent to which even so sane and balanced a thinker as he did not hesitate to go on occasion:

The "instrument of ten strings" on which the Psalmist wanted to praise God becomes in one place the Ten Commandments, made delightful and easy by divine grace or the ten fingers which perform the mission of the will in divine service. On the text "Whereof every one beareth twins" he breaks out, "What twins? Why, the law and the prophets"—whereon hangs all in the life of the believer. "The bread, the fish and the egg" which the child asks of his father in the parable are explained in this way—the bread is the soul, the fish is faith, which lives amid the billows of temptation, and the egg is hope, a something, but not the chicken!

There is no limit to the extravagant excesses of those who indulge in this sort of allegorizing except that imposed by their own imaginations. In allegorization, fancy gets a free rein and frequently runs away with its rider. It would not scruple to compare the moon to green cheese if it suited its purpose. Yet allegory need not be absurd; it can be enlightening. It need not be ridiculous; it can be revealing. Used with discretion and restraint, allegorization may prove to be a valuable visual aid in preaching.

Bunyan, it has been said, "saw principles like men walking in the street." Yes, and he made them walk into his books and into his sermons. We, too, may, so far as we are able, personify and vitalize in our discourses moral qualities and attributes. Only, we must be careful not to overdo it, remembering that there has only been one Bunyan!

We pass now to yet another kind of sermon illustration—the anecdote. What are we to say about this sort of pen-picture? To define it precisely is somewhat difficult, but perhaps a clue to its meaning is provided by its etymology. The English word

65

"anecdote" comes from two Greek words, meaning "not given out," "not published." Originally, therefore, an anecdote was a semiprivate narrative, communicated in the currency of living speech, but not accorded formal, exact, and permanent expression in writing.

That definition would not, of course, apply to many of the tales which we quite properly denominate "anecdotes" today. Thousands of these have been recorded and issued in books. What makes them anecdotes is the fact that they are related of a person or persons unknown, that their dates and precise circumstantial details are indefinite, and that as stories they are in consequence told not because of any special historical or biographical interest attached to them, but simply for their narrative qualities.

To be frank, the anecdote is the Cinderella of the illustration family—a Cinderella with little chance, it seems, of donning the glass slippers. One preacher, for instance, has spoken with curling lip of what he calls "the anecdotal virus," and others point with scorn to ministers whose sermons are liberally besprinkled with illustrations as having entered their "anecdotage." Nor do we forget the modern Mrs. Malaprop who said of a certain preacher: "I don't like his antidotes!"

And, again, as in the case of parables, it is really no wonder that there has been a strong revulsion of feeling against the anecdote. Since the spacious days of Spurgeon, so many amorphous tales have been going the rounds of the churches— some of them sentimental, some of them supposed to be ornamental, but most of them just plain mental—that it is entirely understandable that the luckless listeners should have at any rate inwardly revolted against them. Such tawdry tales are tedious in the extreme, and present-day congregations cannot stomach them.

Notwithstanding all this, the anecdote does have its own humble and unchallengeable place in preaching. Not a few of us, despite all the spurious specimens we have come across, would actually ditto the dictum of Samuel Johnson: "I *love* anecdotes." Was it not George Bernard Shaw who once remarked to H. G. Wells that any man's life story might be told in the form of three typical anecdotes? And did not Paxton Hood go even further and declare that we tend to doubt the very historicity of a person, of whose name we have a record, if no anecdotes are reported about him? Say what we will to the contrary, there are anecdotes which are super-illustrations, and which it would be a million pities to place under interdict where preaching is concerned. Their ancestry may be open to question, their authenticity may be suspect, but their worth as word-pictures is beyond computation.

Here are three of them:

A young man went once into the mountains to pray. It was a fine, still summer morning, and as he climbed upward he saw the peaks surrounding him floodlit with the glory of the dawn. Mounting higher and higher, he raised his eyes heavenward and, with uplifted arms, in passionate prayer, he exclaimed: "More of Thee! More of Thee! More of Thee!" Back from the surrounding summits came the echo: "More of thee! More of thee! More of thee!" It is a parable. If we want more of God, we must give him more of ourselves.

Now, from the point of view of the effectiveness of that anecdote as a sermon illustration, it does not matter tuppence who that young man was; it does not matter what mountain he was climbing; indeed, it does not really matter whether or not the thing ever happened at all. What does matter is the point which the story makes so strikingly and unforgettably. Dare anyone suggest that such an anecdote is unfit for pulpit use?

Or consider a further anecdotal illustration:

There was a lad once who had it in him to be a brilliant violinist. His parents, who were well-to-do, set him to study under a famous maestro. An extraordinarily apt and able pupil, the boy made rapid

67

progress, proving himself in truth little short of a genius. The day came when he was thought sufficiently proficient to give a public recital. A large auditorium was booked for the occasion, the event was given the widest possible publicity, and on the evening of the performance the vast building was packed to capacity. The youthful violinist was advertised to play several pieces. As he rendered the first, his instrument wove into the air a pattern of exquisite sound. The audience was transported and, when he had ended, the applause was tumultuous. But the young violinist did not seem satisfied. Always he kept turning to a point in the gallery as if watching for something. The second piece he rendered with even more feeling and finish and, as the music died away, the cheering was louder still. Yet clearly the young musician was not content with his performance. Anxiously, he went on gazing up to that point in the gallery, as if all his thoughts were focused there. Into the playing of the third piece he poured his very soul, wedding emotional sincerity to manual dexterity, and far surpassing anything he had done before. At the close, the acclamation was terrific. And this time the young violinist was smiling radiantly, for yonder on the gallery was the old maestro, tears streaming down his cheeks, as he clapped with rapturous abandon. It was enough. To the youthful performer all that really mattered was to please the master.

> Men heed thee, love thee, praise thee not?
> The Master praises: what are men? [5]

No one with the least trace of homiletic sensibility can fail to perceive how admirably adapted to sermonic use is that moving narrative. Yet I cannot go on oath that it is true. I cannot identify the young fellow in the story as Paganini or Kreisler or Yehudi Menuhin. But, tell me, what does it signify whether I can or not? Would it greatly enhance the value of the anecdote if I could? Or is it not the case that if we knew for certain that the tale was pure fiction, without a word of truth in it, it would not alter by a hairsbreadth its power over our hearts?

Take one more anecdotal illustration—this time a tale told

[5] Horatius Bonar, "Go, labor on."

by Henry Drummond. He does not indicate its source, and very likely did not know what it was any more than I do, but the story is well worth narrating for its own sake. It is as follows:

A young woman was dying in hospital. She had been a prostitute and was sodden with sin; but, when on her sickbed, she had sought and found forgiveness and cleansing through Christ. The text used in her conversion was: "He was wounded for our transgressions: He was bruised for our iniquities." Rapidly, she grew worse and her friends were hastily sent for. They thought her dead. Presently, however, she opened her eyes, stretched out one hand and with the fore-finger of the other pointed to her palm. "There is no wound there," she said. And then, pointing upward, she added: "He was wounded for my transgressions." For a while she lay quite still, and then again she spoke. Putting her hand to her brow, she said: "There are no thorns there"; and, pointing upward, went on: "He was wounded for my transgressions." Once more her eyes closed and they thought she was gone. But a third time she looked up and, clasping her hands across her breast, she said: "There is no spearwound here"; and, pointing up as before: "He was wounded for my trans-gressions." So saying, she passed into the Unseen.

Here, again, the fact that the name of the unfortunate female in the story is not divulged in no way derogates from the im-pressiveness of the narrative. We are not gripped and touched by the tale just because we happen to recognize the figure who features in it. Were we able definitely to identify her as Nell Gwyn, that would make no appreciable difference to the impact of the narrative upon us. What seizes and holds us is the story itself. The circumstance that its central character is anonymous is almost irrelevant.

Let us not, then, be afraid to retail a good story just because we are not sure of its factuality. Rather let us recall W. R. Maltby's whimsical remark: "I will venture a story, and I know it is true because I made it up myself!" Although not true to fact —to employ a hackneyed but happy distinction—a tale may be true to life. And, if so, it will serve equally well our pictorial purpose in preaching.

Another category into which our sermon illustrations may be sorted is that of *historical happenings*. Lewis Carroll tells us that when Alice fell into the pool of tears and got soaked through, she dried herself by reading a volume of history! It would be tragic if that represented the truth about the readability of the records of our race. Fortunately, it does not. It is only a jest, for history can be in fact one of the most fascinating of studies. Surely that is only what might be expected of the picture book of humanity, the family album of mankind. Would it not be passing strange if, with all that colorful panorama before us, we were not to find in it many a graphic scene and glittering spectacle with which to embellish our sermons?

Glance for a moment at the following examples. (For our present purpose I am assuming the historicity of this first narrative, although there appear to be grave suspicions that it is the product of the fertile Welsh imagination!)

One of the most decisive and epoch-making events in the history of Wales occurred in the middle of the thirteenth century, when Edward I of England, after years of guerilla warfare with the Welsh, entered into peaceful negotiations with their national leaders. Previously, Edward, a man of iron resolution, stamping ruthlessly on everything that stood in his way, had set his heart upon uniting by military action the three kingdoms of Britain under the English crown. He set off by trying to conquer Wales. To start with, he met with stout and stubborn resistance. Commanding the Welsh forces was Llewellyn, Prince of Snowdon, a popular and patriotic figure, who led his men into the mountain fastnesses, where they were practically undefeatable. Before long, however, he was bold enough to join issue with Edward in the open field. A bitter battle ensued and Llewellyn was beaten. His head was severed from his body and sent to London in token of Edward's triumph. But the victory was short-lived. After a brief spell, fighting broke out again, and at last the cunning king contrived a plan by which he hoped to gain by craft what he had failed to compass by main force. Summoning the Welsh chieftains to a conference, he asked them whether they would accept and own abiding allegiance to a prince of his appointing, provided he complied with the following three conditions: He must be the son of a king; he must have been born in their own country; and he must be such a prince as no one could charge with any fault. It was a clever stratagem. The Welsh cheerfully agreed to the terms, feeling doubtless that no prince of that type could anywhere be found. Whereupon Edward exultantly offered them his own son who, unknown to them, had just been born in the Castle of Caernarvon! What could the Welsh do? There was nothing for it but to welcome with as good grace as might be the young prince thus proffered them. So it comes about that to this day the eldest son of the English royal house is called "The Prince of Wales."

Is not that a capital illustration for a Christmas sermon? Not only does it supply the preacher with colorful pictorial material; it even provides him with the three points which classic homiletic usage prescribes.

Another striking and stirring historical illustration is taken from James Scotland's racy and informative little volume *Modern Scotland*. The story presents an illuminative parallel to the suspicion, ingratitude, derision, and downright hostility with which men often greet the glorious offer of the gospel. Here is the narrative:

Late in the month of July, 1707, a troop of dragoons was trotting northwards along a country road in Northumberland. In the midst of them, creaking over the deep dry ruts, went a number of wagons carrying nearly £400,000 worth of gold and exchequer bills, a gift from the English government to their "ancient and inveterate enemies," the Scots, under the terms of the recent Act of Union of the two countries. How did the Scots receive them? Daniel Defoe, the famous author, was in Edinburgh at the time as an English agent. He heard the citizens of the Scottish capital shout that the gold boxes were full of stones and the exchequer bills worthless pieces of paper and "notes on the bank of fancy." They were not content to

71

hiss: they threw stones at the drivers, bank officers and soldiers all the way to the gates of Edinburgh Castle.[6]

Employed in illustration of the texts, "He came unto his own, and his own received him not" (John 1:11), and "Ye will not come to me, that ye might have life" (John 5:40), that word-picture can give point and poignancy to sad facts of our Savior's life, familiarity with which may have blunted the senses of our listeners to their tragedy.

For our final historical illustration in this place consider the following:

There are few more stirring stories than that of the conquest of Quebec. The thrilling incident it recounts occurred on September 13, 1759, when the city fell to a British brigade commanded by General James Wolfe. Under cover of darkness, the invaders sailed up the St. Lawrence River, gave the secret password to the enemy sentries, leapt ashore at a point now known as "Wolfe's Cove" and, filing through a narrow pass, came at last to the Plains of Abraham. Above them frowned the famous "Heights," so steep that even Wolfe's stout heart quailed at the sight of them, so that for a moment he feared that his troops would not be able to scale them. Farther aloft still stood the seemingly impregnable fortress occupied by the French. Could the attackers possibly succeed in capturing so strongly defended a position? Before dawn it was in their hands. The ramparts were reached, the guards surprised and overpowered, the garrison utterly defeated, and the British jubilantly took possession of the fort. But in the action Wolfe was mortally wounded. Three times that night he had fallen before the enemy's gunfire, and the third time he fell to rise no more. Just before he breathed his last, they brought him news of the battle. A faint smile flickered on his bloodless lips. "The victory is ours!" he gasped; and then, rallying all his forces to frame the pathetic appeal, he added: "Oh, keep it!"

Used in conjunction with I Cor. 15:57, "Thanks be to God, which giveth us the victory through our Lord Jesus Christ," this

[6] (London: G. Bell & Sons, 1953), p. 1.

word-picture can be very effective, stressing as it does the often overlooked point that, although Christ has won moral and spiritual victory for us at the cost of his Cross, it is our personal responsibility, by active resistance to evil and in reliance on his grace and strength, to keep that victory. To a discourse on that topic this incident from history would form a fine and fitting frontispiece.

In sorting out our sermon illustrations we are almost sure to find that by far the largest number of them may be classified, in one way or another, as *biographical episodes*. Biography positively teems with telling pictorial instances presenting themselves in shoals for our preaching purposes.

From my own stock I select three striking examples.

The first is taken from that enthralling book, *Portrait and Pageant*, by Frank O. Salisbury, the eminent artist. It describes how he set about painting his celebrated study of John Wesley. Collecting as much material about Wesley as he could, in the form of relics, pictures, and even a very lifelike bust loaned by the Victoria and Albert Museum, he examined them intently and sought to build up in his mind a composite idea of the appearance of his subject and of the impression which he must have made on his contemporaries. Still he felt that there was something lacking, that he needed a living model, bearing a strong likeness to Wesley and of about the age at which he wanted to portray him, seventy-five. One man he knew would, he decided, best "fill the bill." That man was Charles Voysey, the architect. Salisbury approached him and asked if he would do him the favor. "He looked upon me in astonishment," wrote the painter, "and said nothing would give him greater pleasure, for he belonged to the Wesley family." Salisbury had not known that, but the undoubted similarity of facial features was a family resemblance.

Suppose that sometime in a sermon we are concerned to illustrate the contention that likeness to God results from and is conditional upon receiving the life of God—a thought implicit

73

in John 1:12: "As many as received him, to them gave he power to become the sons of God"—how more aptly and appropriately could we do so than by relating some such topical instance as that?

The second biographical illustration might conveniently be coupled with Matt. 6:6: "But thou, when thou prayest, enter into thy closet, and when thou hast shut thy door, pray to thy Father which is in secret; and thy Father which seeth in secret shall reward thee." The incident narrated hereunder would form an excellent word-picture for a sermon on that text:

Many years ago a young shoemaker was sitting one day with his fiancée on the circular bench which surrounds the interior of the Whispering Gallery under the dome of St. Paul's Cathedral, London. The young man was mournfully explaining to his sweetheart that, business being very bad, he had no money with which to buy a supply of leather and was consequently out of work, and so would be unable to marry her on the date which they had previously fixed. The girl began to cry when she heard the sad news. Opposite them on the gallery, 190 feet away, sat an old gentleman; and, around the wall of the dome whose acoustics are so marvelous, was carried to his ears the conversation of the two young lovers. When they got up to go home, the old gentleman followed them, without their knowing it, to the shoemaker's shop, whither he arranged to have a large consignment of leather sent right away. Duly, the hides arrived and the shoemaker was delirious with delight, although he had no clue as to whence they had come and only accepted them after being assured that they really were for him. Immediately, he set to work; his business prospered and soon, the financial obstacle to his marriage having been removed, he was able to wed the girl of his choice. Not until a long while afterward did he find out—and even then only by accident—that his mysterious benefactor had been none other than the great Prime Minister, William Ewart Gladstone.

The third illustration in this class is connected with Copenhagen. It is a scintillating episode in the life of the great Danish sculptor, Thorwaldsen. Here is the word-picture:

74

Bertel Thorwaldsen was born in Denmark, the son of a poor Icelander. He became one of the world's greatest sculptors. Most of his life was spent in Italy, though he did live also for a while in Greece and in Switzerland. And always, wherever he was, he spent his time modeling and chiseling masterpieces of sculpture. As his days drew in, his heart turned home and he resolved to return to his native land. But he did not do so empty-handed. With him he brought many of the magnificent statues he had carved, or the plaster casts from which he had modeled them. Chartering a fleet of vessels, he took home to Copenhagen the treasures of his genius. It was a great day for him and a great day for the Danish capital. Flags flew bravely from the mastheads of the palace and other public buildings, bells pealed merrily forth, and trumpets sounded to celebrate the occasion. Out from the wharf floated a flotilla of gaily decorated barges, in one of which sailed the king and other members of the royal family, while another carried members of the senate and other officers of state, prominent citizens, and so on. Amid scenes of rapturous rejoicing, Thorwaldsen presented his masterpieces to the king. Then, taken ashore, the statues were placed on open wagons and drawn through the crowded streets of the capital to the admiration and acclamation of the populace. Finally, they were taken to the museum where they were placed on permanent exhibition.

We might turn that to good use in a sermon on Jude 24-25: "Now unto him that is able to keep you from falling, and to present you faultless before the presence of his glory with exceeding joy, to the only wise God our Saviour, be glory and majesty, dominion and power, both now and ever. Amen." The heart thrills to the thought of Jesus molding and fashioning the lives of men and women in all parts of the world, shaping them to moral perfection, and purposing to present them at last without flaw to the eternal King amid the exulting hosts of heaven. And where could one find a finer picture of that crowning hour than in this episode from the career of Thorwaldsen?

Only one more type of sermon illustration yet abides our question—that of *personal reminiscence*. From the deep pools of our subconscious minds we can fish up many a flashing recollection, something we have seen or heard or read, something which we can profitably employ as pictorial sermon material.

Specimen number one links up well with John 10:2-5: "He that entereth in by the door is the shepherd of the sheep: To him the porter openeth . . . ; and he calleth his own sheep by name, and leadeth them out. . . . The sheep follow him: for they know his voice. And a stranger will they not follow, but will flee from him: for they know not the voice of strangers." The word-painting takes this form:

Some years ago I lodged with a well-to-do farmer near the town of Fielding in New Zealand. His home was situated in the midst of undulating country, dotted here and there with clumps of stunted trees. At the front of the house there was a veranda overlooking a large paddock in the center of which was a bush-covered knoll. One lovely morning my host conducted me on to the veranda and bade me cup my hands to my lips and shout as loudly as I could: "Come along! Come along! Come along!" I did, but nothing happened. The paddock in front of me seemed as empty as before. There was absolutely no sign of animal life of any kind. My friend smiled. "Now," he said, "watch this." Then he did precisely what I had done, calling out the same words, at the same vocal pitch. And instantly from all over the vast field sheep began to appear, and before long several scores of them had gathered just below the veranda. "There is an illustration for you," remarked my friend. "A stranger will they not follow; for they know not the voice of strangers." He was right.

Now for specimen number two of this variety of illustration:

On the night of Good Friday, 1962, I crossed from Glasgow to Belfast on the motor vessel "Irish Coast." I had provisionally booked a berth; but, the sky being fairly clear and the moon at the full, I resolved to stay up all night in the hope of catching sight by moonlight of the Isle of Arran, for me an island of many memories. When, however, between one and two in the morning, the ship reached the point at which, standing there on the moonlit deck and straining my eyes in an effort to pierce the darkness, I had counted on getting a glimpse of the island, I discovered to my intense disappointment that, although the heavens were bare, I could not make Arran out at all because of a low mist hanging over it. Try as I might, I was unable to penetrate the gloom. Then, all at once, the captain on the bridge spotted me, a lone figure on the windy deck, and sent down a sailor, kindly inviting me to join him on the bridge. Gladly I accepted the invitation; and, as I entered the control room, he said, pointing to the radar apparatus: "I don't suppose you've seen anything like that before." "No," I replied, "I haven't." "Well," he went on, "have a good look at it now. See—there in bright outline is the Island of Arran, which we are just passing. This is Brodick, that is Lamlash, and yonder is Whiting Bay." "Captain," I said, "I gave up a night's sleep on the off chance of seeing Arran; but, despite the good general visibility, I was afraid the sight was going to be denied me." "You don't say," he ejaculated. "Yes," I continued, "and yet now, sir, thanks to your kindness, I *have* seen it on this illuminated screen!"

And, even as I made the remark, into my mind slipped that great word of the apostle: "Eye hath not seen, nor ear heard . . . the things which God hath prepared for them that love him. But God hath revealed them unto us by his Spirit" (I Cor. 2:9, 10).

To us the future seems mistily mysterious. We cannot clearly survey its shadowy shore. Its reality eludes us. Despite our dim and defective apprehension of it, however, it really is there; and high hours come when the Captain calls us onto the bridge and when, notwithstanding the darkness of doubt and our finite ignorance, on the radar screen of faith we view the land that is fairer than day.

Specimen number three of this class of illustration is of a poignantly personal character. It is a tear-stained page torn from the book of memory. Natural reserve and reticence would make one want to draw a veil over it; yet to be silent about it were surely to have suffered in vain. This, then, is the little story:

Never shall I forget the day when our baby son, only a few weeks old, lay dangerously ill. His mother and I were praying desperately that he might be spared to us, but it was not to be. To everybody but ourselves—blinded by love and hope—it was plain that the end was near. Since there was no help for it, we were bidden to pray,

77

"Thy will be done," and resign ourselves to the inevitable. I simply could not bring myself to say it. When I tried, the words stuck in my throat. One evening, after weary days and nights of watchfulness, it was suggested that as a break in the sad vigil, I should go for a short walk. I did. Wandering about disconsolately for a while, I drifted at last into a religious service, where, as I discovered, a Salvation Army captain was about to give the address. She took two texts—or rather, to be more exact, she took one text which is found in two places—and she began by asking us to consider the text in both settings. The text was, "Thy will be done," and she pointed out that not only does this sentence form part of the Lord's Prayer, but that it was also used by Jesus himself during his desperate hour of supplication in Gethsemane. Listening to this, I could not but feel that it was startlingly relevant to my immediate situation; but when, in closing, the captain went on to relate the following incident from her personal experience, the tension became for me well-nigh unbearable. "A few years ago," she said, "when I was an officer attached to the Hull Corps, I was visiting one day in a poor quarter of the town and called on a woman who, although once a loyal soldier in the local citadel, had gone back on the vows she made at her enlistment. I asked her why, and she gave me a very unexpected and touching reply. 'Did you see a youth at the door as you came in?' she inquired. 'Yes.' 'And did you notice anything peculiar about him?' 'No.' 'Well, that boy is an imbecile! Fifteen years ago, when he was an infant, the Lord wanted to take him; but I clung to him and would not let him go, refusing to say, Thy will be done. I would gladly say it now, but it is too late. That is why you do not see me at the citadel any more. Understand?' "

Hearing this story, as the captain unfolded it, I was moved to the depths of my being and melted into submision. "Lord," I prayed, "if you want to take the little chap, I don't want to keep him. Thy will be done." Next day the baby died.

Life is like that. As it goes on, it brings us many baffling and painful experiences which furnish us with firsthand illustrations for our sermons; and, among all the word-pictures we use, none are more powerful or more appealing, and none find their way more readily to the hearers' hearts.

3

Tracking Them Down

Man is a born hunter. The instinct displays itself in widely diverse ways—in stamp collecting and in stalking big game; in searching for bargains in shops and markets and in whaling amid the white seas of frozen zones; in archaeological research and in dogging the viruses of dread diseases. However it manifests itself, the thing is there. Man is a born hunter.

In us preachers this passion for hunting assumes various forms —we have to seek for sermonic materials of different kinds— but the aspect of the quest with which we are here principally concerned is that connected with the discovery of word-pictures.

Where are we to find them? An obvious answer is supplied by books of quotable anecdotes, which spare the busy minister the trouble of personally tracking illustrations down, much as a visit to the fish market or the butcher may save one the effort of faring forth with rod or gun.

What are we to say about such omnibus volumes? There is no disguising the fact that many of the homiletic experts are dead against them. "I once inherited a book entitled A Thousand Things To Say in Sermons," remarks J. H. Hammerton. "I am glad to be able to report," he adds complacently, "that I have not said one of them." "Avoid all these despicable substitutes for your own labour," advises G. Johnstone Jeffrey, "which may be summarily comprehended under the titles Tools for Teachers and Plums for Preachers." W. E. Sangster is even more brutally outspoken. He bids us burn them or send them to be repulped!

79

Yet surely that is taking things too far. Such eminent preachers, speaking from the opulence of an autumnal fertility, when, after long years of patient garnering, they have acquired an ample stock of illustrative matter, have evidently forgotten what it felt like to be a young and inexperienced fledgling in the art of sermon making with no comfortable "nest egg" to resort to in emergency.

Not a few notable ministers have indeed testified that such manuals proved of profit to them in the opening stages of their careers. Among these was no less distinguished a practitioner in the preacher's craft than Adam Burnet. "You may need," he says, "especially in your early days, some help with illustrations. . . . I am not ashamed to say that in my first ministry I used an old book called *Tools for Teachers*."

On the other hand, Clarence E. Macartney recommends that the use of such works be reserved for the minister's more discriminating maturity. "If I were to prescribe for the young preacher," he observes, "I might well advise him not to buy books of illustrations during perhaps the first five years of his ministry. After that it is safe for him to do so, perhaps wise, for then he has more discrimination, more self-dependence, and can separate the wheat from the chaff in a book of illustrations."

Where experts differ it is dangerous to dogmatize. All the same, I do think that recourse to such collections of illustrations may legitimately be had at any time in a preacher's ministry, subject to three provisos. The first is that the illustrations be not just lifted out of the books in question, but be used simply as prompters. To seek to patch up a discourse with ready-made pieces of pictorial material is despicable; but surely there can be no valid objection to employing an encyclopedia of anecdotes as a promptuary to "spark off" the illustrative potential in one's own mind!

Something of this sort happened to me not long ago. At the time I was particularly interested in the Pauline theme of adoption. That was the topic on which I intended to speak in a forth-coming sermon. Searching for suitable word-pictures, I thumbed through a published collection of anecdotes and came upon an allusion to H. M. Stanley in which the fact was mentioned that he was an adopted child. Up to that time I had not read the autobiography of H. M. Stanley, the British explorer of Africa, although I had it on my bookshelf. I took it down and made some fascinatingly relevant discoveries. Stanley's real name was John Rowlands; he was born in a cottage in Wales; his father died a few days before his birth and shortly afterward his mother absconded, and eventually the poor child was consigned to the workhouse. "In my earliest dreams and fancies," wrote Stanley, "I had often imagined what kind of a boy I should be with a father or mother." He went to sea and in the course of his travels met in New Orleans the kind benefactor whose adoption of him revolutionized his life. "His reception of me was so paternal that the Prodigal Son could not have been more delighted," he records. "He was saying, with some emotion, that my future should be his charge. . . . I broke down. It was the only tender action I had ever known." Here was precisely what I had been looking for, perhaps as fine an illustration on the topic as can be found in all literature. Yet that encyclopedia of anecdotes did not "give" me the word-painting; it only put me in the way of getting it for myself.

And this brings me to my next proviso. It is this: If such omnibus volumes of illustrations are to be utilized to the maximum advantage, it is advisable that before using any item we should take pains to find out as much as we can about its background. To acquire a reputation for wide culture by merely mentioning famous names in the pulpit, quoting sayings, or narrating incidents borrowed from books we have never ourselves read is comparatively easy; but it has one grave hazard. Someday, while doing so, we may inadvertently betray our ignorance and make ourselves laughingstocks. An uneducated Welsh preacher I know did exactly that. Having noticed in a volume of quotations certain noble lines ascribed to Scotland's national bard, and being in blissful ignorance of the poet's character, the preacher introduced the citation into a sermon not long afterward with the sublimely gauche preamble: "As that grand old Scottish *saint,* Robert Burns, has said . . . !"

My third proviso is that the thing be not done too often. When that happens, our favorite treasury of illustrations is liable to take the place of the Bible as our sermon sourcebook. One can become so shallowly topical that one is always on the trail of a tale when one ought to be mining in the Word of God. Never must we forget that the message should ever be paramount, a message firmly founded on and fastened to the scripture, and that the illustrative matter in the sermon can only warrantably be included in it if it serves the interests of the truth under review.

Subject, as I say, to these three provisos, we may give our blessing to the use of such encyclopedias of illustrations. But, after all, books like these are at best but interim aids or helps in emergency. Beyond doubt the writer *did* have a point who maintained that "culling illustrations is an art, recording them a discipline and an industry, but ready-made examples stultify the imagination and usually lack freshness and character." To which one must in honesty and fairness append the footnote: "It is surprising how few really workable illustrations are to be found in a large book of illustrations."

For the most part, then, we shall have to look elsewhere for fields in which to track down our pen-pictures. What are those fields? They are as wide as life itself; but we may perhaps fruitfully remind ourselves of several different sources from which illustrations may be drawn.

We will consider them in swift succession.

Pride of place must, of course, be given to the Bible. Later in our study we shall be thinking about literature in general as an inexhaustible magazine of pictorial materials; such, however, is

82

the towering supremacy of the Bible over every other volume that it is really in a class by itself and so calls for special treatment.

Indisputably, the finest omnibus book of illustrations on biblical themes is the Bible itself. Just as we can only see the sun in its own light, so nothing illuminates scripture like scripture. There is hardly a page of Holy Writ which does not contain a picture in which the homiletic mind may discern symbolic significance and illustrative value. Aspiring to preach pictorially, we have here an ample acreage in which to prosecute our search.

The appeal of stories from the Bible, and their usableness as visual aids in preaching are vastly enhanced and extended nowadays by virtue of the fact that so few of one's listeners are likely to be familiar with them. Time was, not so long ago, when they were too well known to be legal tender in the pulpit. Employing them then, a preacher ran a certain risk, for most people were able to foresee the end of the narrative from the beginning, and so the stories, in the telling, lost much of that element of suspense and surprise to which tales largely owe their effect.

Now things are otherwise. To vast numbers of people in our so-called Christian communities the Bible is almost as much a mystery as the Koran—and seems almost as irrelevant. There are countless thousands to whom, as David Read remarks, "Genesis is only a biological term"; multitudes whose limited knowledge of the Word of God is as narrow as that of the ignoramus of whom Andrew Blackwood reports that he thought Sodom and Gomorrah were husband and wife! On a wide scale today people have forsaken Holy Writ for unholy rot.

Among those who still keep up a nominal and formal connection with some place of worship the situation is not much better. "Even in churches where Bibles are provided so that the congregation can follow the readings from Scripture," slyly comments John B. Nettleship, "there is an inordinate amount of page-turning when the preacher announces a reading from the Book of Ruth or the Epistle to Philemon."

83

In itself the position is tragic. Yet it *does* offer us modern ministers a distinct advantage over our predecessors so far as the use in our sermons of the illustrative content of the Bible is concerned. The finest stories ever written are within the pages of the Word of God, and if the people of our time are not familiar with them, so much the worse for the people of our time—but so much the better for us as pictorial preachers.

What an invaluable preaching asset these biblical stories can be! "There are no illustrations," says Spurgeon, "as good as those from Scripture." In a recent book Robert Menzies eloquently makes the same point: "The Scriptures are shot through and through with flesh-and-blood portraits, with historical situations, with analogies from the natural world, with sparkling similes and metaphors, which flash like the jewelled hilt of an Oriental sword." With such incalculable funds of illustration at our disposal, we cannot fail to find in the Bible something to fit each emergent pictorial requirement. We may use the Bible to illustrate the Bible.

It is patent from the Old Testament that God himself used ilustrations when conveying his message to mankind. So the prophets assure us. On page after page they describe how the Almighty communicated to them creative conceptions of his mind and heart and will. Jeremiah saw baskets of figs; Ezekiel saw a valley of dry bones; Amos saw a wall and a plumbline; Zechariah saw a man with a measuring line.

And, in their turn, the prophets themselves, when transmitting their revelations to us, likewise adopt the pictorial approach. Jeremiah ties a linen girdle about his loins, a girdle which for a while he is forbidden to wash, and which he hides in a rocky hole by the River Euphrates, afterward recovering it; Ezekiel draws on a tile a diagram of Jerusalem, places it on the ground, and builds mimic fortifications around it, employing an iron pan to stand for the wall of iron between himself and the city (perhaps, as John Dow suggests, the first anticipation of the Iron

Curtain), and makes pretense of laying siege to the miniature capital; Hosea plays in real life the pathetic part of a deserted husband buying back his wayward wife for fifteen pieces of silver, and so on.

A particularly rich treasury of illustrations lies open to us in the biographies of the Bible. Of these Alexander Whyte, George Matheson, F. B. Meyer, Mackintosh Mackay, and Clovis G. Chappell—to name only a few—have made free and frequent use in their ministries. Brief sketches such as those of Micah of Ephraim in Judges 17 and 18, or that of Onesimus in the epistle to Philemon, are practically ready-made picture-sermons, while from the more extended and detailed accounts of the lives of such characters as Joseph and Jeremiah almost limitless illustrative materials may be extracted. The book of Ruth is a charming pastoral idyll, that of Jonah a superb piece of missionary propaganda, and that of Job a magnificent drama dealing with one of the most poignant and intractable problems of human existence.

But the pictorial values of the Bible are not confined to the Old Testament. In the New Testament also the illustrative strain is very strong—the exquisite parables and analogies of the Gospels, the glitteringly brilliant historical episodes of the book of Acts, the striking figures in the Epistles, and the gorgeous imagery and colorful tableaux of the Book of Revelation being witness. Surely we have here an exhaustless array of pictorial possibility.

From this bewilderingly vast assortment of word-pictures I pick three for special mention.

Suppose we want a biblical illustration for a discourse on the text, "God was in Christ, reconciling the world unto himself" (II Cor. 5:19). Our plan is to show, as far as we humanly can, how much it cost God to redeem our race. Where are we likely to find anything closer to our need than that moving and dramatic narrative (unfolded in Gen. 22:1-14) of the pilgrimage of Abraham and Isaac to the land of Moriah? Painting as graphic a description as we can of that heart-shattering journey, we may cause our people to overhear, as it were, God's beloved Son crying, as he climbs the hill of Calvary: "Father, here is the wood —this grisly cross upon my back—and here is the fire—the love blazing in my heart—but where is the lamb for the burnt offering?" And then we may bid our hearers listen awestruck to the voice of John the Baptist booming down the years: "Behold the Lamb of God which taketh away the sin of the world" (John 1:29).

Or suppose we have in prospect a sermon on Rom. 8:28: "And we know that all things work together for good to them that love God, to them who are the called according to his purpose." Our aim is to point out how, in spite of human ignorance, folly, and sin, God directs the happenings of life for the highest welfare of those who love him and strive to do his will. Was there ever a recorded career better adapted to do just that than the career of Joseph? All the reverses and tragedies, the conflicts and struggles, of his checkered history, were compelled to subserve the divine purpose for his life, chiseling and chastening his character and preparing him to be the possessor of princely power. So far as his experience went, all things, literally all things —all the dark, mysterious, enigmatic things—did work together for good. Was he basely sold by his own brothers to a band of Bedouins? That was God's way of getting him to Egypt, the scene of his subsequent distinction and success. Was he falsely slandered and flung into jail? That was God's mode of bringing him into contact with the royal butler, who at last, albeit tardily, was the means of his recognition, release, and promotion. Was the land to which he went laid low by famine? That was God's mode of putting his brothers and his father into touch with him again and of healing the old sad breach between them. All Joseph's adversities were advances, every seeming setback proved a forward move; and when, in old age, Joseph came to review the

long track he had traveled, he was keen enough to perceive this
and magnanimous enough to admit it even to those who had so
shamefully wronged him: "As for you, ye thought evil against
me; but God meant it unto good" (Gen. 50:20).

Or, again, on another occasion our theme may be the fact
that, to the Christian, reinforcements are always available, when
he requires them, in the realm unseen. Taking as text Heb.
11:27, "He endured, as seeing him who is invisible," and casting
about in the Bible for some luminous illustration to light up our
topic, our thoughts turn, as if by instinct, to a stirring story recorded in II Kings 6:8-23. It recounts the experience of Elisha
and his manservant when they awoke one morning in Dothan
to find themselves surrounded by the serried ranks of Syria. We
may, if we wish, paraphrase the story something like this:

The King of Syria had been planning an attack on Israel; but
every time he did so, his strategy was anticipated and the assault forestalled. Suspecting a leakage of official secrets among his privy counselors, he summoned them together and peremptorily demanded:
"Will ye not show me which of us is for the King of Israel?" Following the question, there was, we may well imagine, an awkward
silence for a time, while every man searched the others' faces. Then
one of the counselors ventured to reply: "None, my Lord, O King,
but Elisha the prophet that is in Israel, telleth the King of Israel
the things that thou speakest in thy bedchamber." At once action was
taken. A detachment of troops was sent to arrest the man of God.
Thus it came about that when Elisha's servant went one morning to
the rooftop of their house in Dothan, he got a sudden shock. The
place was surrounded by Syrian hordes. Hastening into the presence
of the prophet, the servant threw up his hands in terror and dismay:
"Alas, my master," he cried, "how shall we do?" Elisha's answer was
a prayer. "Lord, open his eyes." And instantly the youth saw what
he had not seen before, ceased to be victimized by the materially
visible, realizing that his master and he had secret allies in the supernatural world, and that round about them were "the chariots of
Israel and the horsemen thereof." Upon his wondering view broke

in the powers of the world unseen. Just then he could have made his own words written centuries later by Charles Wesley:

> Lo! to faith's enlightened sight,
> All the mountain flames with light;
> Hell is nigh, but God is nigher,
> Circling us with hosts of fire.[1]

There we have three sparkling examples of how impressively and improvingly the Bible can be used to illustrate the Bible, one part casting a revealing radiance on another part, the Old Testament illuminating the New and the New Testament the Old. Nowhere is there a richer literary repository of sermon illustrations than the Word of God. Besides being a uniquely divine book, it is an intensely human book, packed with graphic scenes, swift-moving incidents, and lifelike portraits each capable of somehow ministering to the preacher's pictorial effectiveness. He need not lack for exciting word-pictures.

Another field in which we may ferret for sermon-pictures is nature. Here, again, we have a boundless store of illustrative materials. Nature has been called that "Older Testament, that Bible of pictures"—an apt and striking description. R. F. Horton contended that "God Himself has published the best book of illustrations for preaching in nature." Charles Kingsley tells how

> Nature, the old nurse, took
> The child upon her knee,
> Saying, Here is a story-book
> Thy Father hath written for thee.

And G. H. Morrison beautifully observed: "There is another book written by the same finger and inspired. It too has its Genesis and we call it January. It too has its Revelation and we call it June."

---

[1] From *Hymns and Sacred Poems*, 1740. "To be sung in a tumult."

Now, it cannot be disputed that in some of its aspects nature wears what has been termed a "God-denying look": equally certainly, however, it has a "God-implying look." Throughout the ages philosophers and savants of all kinds have sought to solve the problem of its seeming dualism. That has been the radical riddle of history, a mystery which from time immemorial has haunted and mesmerized the human mind. By it the wisest and the best men of the world have been profoundly perplexed and disturbed. Nature has conveyed to them contrary and even contradictory impressions. They have thought of the milk in a mother's breast and then of the venom in a serpent's prong; they have thought of the gentle lamb and then of the ferocious tiger; they have thought of the still and lovely summer and then of winter, that devil's carnival; and they have been completely at a loss, so far as their unaided human reason reached, in trying to determine which of the two represents ultimate reality.

The dilemma has been admirably expressed thus by a gifted writer: "We have, on the one hand, the subtle fragrance of the violet, and on the other, the horrible fangs of the viper; we have the delightful trill of the lark, and the blooded beak of the vulture; we have the tender grace of the gazelle, and the dripping tusks of the wolf."

God-denying or God-implying—which is it? Surely it is both and so leaves room for faith.

Naturally, it will be to its God-implying facets that we shall turn most frequently in our quest of word-paintings. Contemplating nature, we shall be constrained to echo the language of Paul: "The invisible things . . . from the creation of the world are clearly seen, being understood by the things that are made, even his eternal power and Godhead" (Rom. 1:20). To us the visible will be a sacrament of the invisible, the seen a symbol of the unseen, the natural an interpretative reflection of the supernatural. "The world below me," said Spurgeon, "is a glass in which I see the world above." Part of our task as pictorial

THE ART OF ILLUSTRATING SERMONS

preachers is, in Shakespeare's phrase, "to hold the mirror up to nature," so that men may see not nature only, but nature's God. In choosing examples of nature illustrations, the only embarrassment one suffers is the embarrassment of riches.

Take two only.

Consider this exquisite instance from the works of A. J. Gordon. Touching on John 3:30, "He must increase, but I must decrease," the celebrated preacher painted this fine picture:

In the part of New England where I spend my summer holidays I have seen a parable of nature which sets forth the truth of this text. It is an example of natural grafting. Two little saplings grew up side by side. Through the action of the wind they crossed each other. By and by the bark of each became wounded and the sap began to mingle until on some still day, they became united together. This process went on more and more and gradually they were firmly compacted. Then the stronger began to absorb the life of the weaker. It grew larger and larger, while the other grew smaller and smaller, withering and declining till it finally dropped away and disappeared. And now there are two trunks at the bottom and only one at the top. Death has taken away the one, life has triumphed in the other. There was a time when you and Jesus Christ met. The wounds of your penitent heart began to knit up with the wounds of His broken heart, and you were united to Christ. Where are you now? Are the two lives running parallel, or has the word been accomplished in you, "He must increase, but I must decrease"? [2]

Or consider this memorable instance from a book called Plant Hunter's Paradise by the renowned explorer and botanist, F. Kingdon Ward. It describes the tragic deterioration which befalls trees in the Burmese jungle when left in isolation from their companions:

[2] Ernest B. Gordon, Adoniram Judson Gordon (New York: Fleming H. Revell Co., 1896), p. 285.

90

Here and there solitary trees are left standing close by the road, either to support the telegraph wire or for some other reason; but almost every one I noticed was almost dead or dying. What is the reason? Probably trees grow in the forest which out in the open cannot survive, lacking the protection of their fellows. At first they strive for immortality by changing their habits, and trees evergreen in the forest become deciduous in the open; but gradually they wilt and perish.

Would not that be a splendid illustration for a sermon on Rom. 14:7? "None of us liveth to himself." It could equally appositely be paneled into a discourse on Heb. 10:25: "Not forsaking the assembling of ourselves together, as the manner of some is." The title of such an address might well be: "The High Cost of Nonchurchgoing."

A further broad field in which we may forage for sermon illustrations is science. As we go in search of pictorial preaching matter, there opens up before us in this sphere a world of dazzling wonders. Science immeasurably heightens man's powers of observation and investigation, vastly widening the area of inquiry and research. Galaxies and constellations invisible to the naked eye swim into the ken of the astronomer in his observatory. Minute organisms, too tiny for unaided inspection, yield up their mysteries to the microscope. Records, indecipherable by the untutored mind, stand forth from the rocks boldly legible to the geologist. Every branch of natural exploration is absolutely brimful of illustrations brilliantly illuminative of spiritual truth.

I offer three samples.

The first is an almost incredible illustration of the phenomenal power of prayer. This version of it I borrow from a striking sermon by Cyril H. Jones:

The person concerned is a scientist, a man who had been almost a devout atheist. Doing research work in a pathological laboratory, along with other doctors, he attempted to find the wavelength of the human brain. They discovered a whole channel of wavelengths—

91

and each channel had so much room that the different wavelength of each individual brain is farther separated in identity than the fingerprints on each individual's hand. This scientist wanted to experiment, to discover what took place in the human brain at the moment of transition from life to death. A lady was selected who had a disease of the brain. This disease affected the balance of the body only. In every other way she was exceptionally brilliant. But her family did not want the trouble of caring for her, and being on the point of death she was accepted as a patient in this research hospital. The necessary wires were connected to her room, to ascertain what would take place; also a small microphone, about the size of a penny, was installed, in case she had anything to say. Five scientists were grouped in an adjoining room—five tough, hardened men, from a religious point of view. One of the instruments they watched had a needle pointing to "O" in the center. To the right the scale registered five hundred points positive; to the left, five hundred points negative. Previously this same instrument had registered the power used by a fifty kilowatt broadcasting station in sending a message round the world. The needle had registered nine points positive. As the last moments of this woman's earthly life arrived, she began to pray aloud and praise God. She asked Him to be merciful to those who had despitefully used her. Then she reaffirmed her faith in God. She praised Him and thanked Him for His power in her, and for her knowledge of His reality. Then she told God how much she loved Him, and was looking forward to seeing Him face to face. The scientists had been so engrossed in this prayer—an unexpected situation—that they had forgotten their experiment. They looked at each other, tears streaming down their faces. The particular scientist we are thinking about said afterwards: "I had not shed tears since I was a child." Suddenly, they heard a clicking sound, and turning to their instruments found that this particular instrument was registering a positive five hundred, and desperately trying to go higher! By actual instrumentation these scientists had recorded that the brain of a woman, alone and dying, in communication with God, had registered more than fifty-five times the power used by a fifty kilowatt station in sending a message round the world! If ever we needed proof of the power of prayer, surely this is it! The faith of

92

this dying woman and her prayer to God resulted in the conversion of the atheistic scientist.[3]

Our second scientific illustration is another consummate example by Leslie Weatherhead. Notice how perfectly it lights up his contention that conformity to the unfolding will of God is the secret of personal serenity. No finer or fitter figure for the purpose could possibly be devised. Here it is:

There is a good illustration for us in the way an airman finds his way home. A radio beam is sent out from his own home station, and once in that beam he has only to follow it to find his way. If he goes out of that directing beam a buzzer sounds in his earphones, telling him clearly enough: "You are going wrong. You must get back until all is quiet." In the home beam there is peace. I think it is not stretching the illustration to say that God sends out, as it were, a beam of direction—namely, his will for us in those circumstances in which we find ourselves—and as long as we keep in his will there is peace. It is when we go out of it or cannot find it—and this can be our case sometimes, however hard we try, as I know to my sorrow—that disturbance and unrest are set up in our minds.[4]

Most impressive and suggestive of all such illustrations to me, however, is the following masterpiece by W. L. Watkinson. It is designed to illustrate the moral dualism of human nature, that internecine strife which Paul describes so graphically in Rom. 7:7-24, and it is difficult to see how any other word-picture could have done it better:

Some misguided scientists have recently succeeded in producing what has been called a diabolical fad. By grafting a portion of one insect upon the body of another, they were able to make new organisms. The result, however, is hideous in the extreme. The grafting is done when the creature is in the pupa state. The insect-grafter

[3] Christian World Pulpit, June 9, 1960.
[4] The Will of God (Nashville: Abingdon Press, 1944), p. 49.

93

may commence work on either the chrysalis or the perfect insect itself; but the chrysalis or grub of the insect offers the best facilities. The vivisector takes the pupa of a spider and, by a delicate surgical operation, grafts it upon the pupa of a fly and when the freak has passed the chrysalis state and merged into a perfect insect, we have a monster indeed. We may fancy the strange and distressing conflict which ensues within the violated organism—the clash of irreconcilable impulse and instinct in a creature compounded of, say, butterfly and spider—a passion for the sunshine and a love of darkness, a longing for roses and a thirst for blood, demanding inconsistent satisfaction —the creature perplexed within itself, afraid of itself, devouring itself.[5]

Because of the prevailing temper of our time, illustrations drawn from the domain of the sciences are likely to exercise a powerful influence over people today.

There are, however, two perils peculiar to the use of them against which we ought ever to be on our guard. One is that they have a habit of becoming dated very quickly. The march of scientific progress is so swift that one needs to keep abreast of it if one is not, perhaps unsuspectingly, to employ illustrations based on supposed facts, which have been found not to be facts at all and so discarded.

Another peril associated with the use of scientific illustrations is that they are apt to betray one into what has been called "the sin of the specialist"—that of taking for granted in our people a familiarity with technological jargon which many of them do not possess. Let us see to it that our scientific illustrations are up-to-date and that they do not cause us to lapse into this discourteous and inconsiderate practice.

Stepping over a further stile, we pass into yet another field in which we may stalk our sermon illustrations—that of art. What a wide terrain here awaits our exploration, and how rewarding the chase is likely to be! Thinking of the imperishable masterpieces which adorn the walls of the great galleries of the world

[5] *The Bane and the Antidote* (London: Epworth Press, n.d.), pp. 3-4.

and of the excellent reproductions of such works now in wide
and inexpensive circulation, we are astounded at the extent and
the exhaustlessness of the possibilities. Is there not in this field
alone sufficient pictorial material to supply our preaching requirements for a lifetime?

Needless to say, this type of illustration possesses strong popular appeal. There is a memorable passage in Harry Emerson
Fosdick's autobiography, *The Living of These Days*, in which
he testifies to the profound and ineffaceable impression made
upon him in youth by a now familiar picture. "I still recall that
awestruck hour," he writes, "when Munkacsy's painting 'Christ
before Pilate' was exhibited in Buffalo and my father and I went
to see it. Something indescribable and unforgettable happened
inside of me that day." Obviously, of course, not even the ablest
preacher can reasonably expect, by a bare description of such
canvases, to exert upon his people an influence at all commen-
surate with that produced by the canvases themselves. Still, however conscious of our limitations, if we study the paintings closely and sensitively and if we are not utterly destitute of some
facility in the choice and use of words, we shall probably contrive to convey to the minds of our hearers a sense of what the
pictures are really like of sufficient vividness and verisimilitude
to serve our homiletic purpose.

Permit me to hang up for inspection three such works of art.

Examine, to start with, a canvas by G. F. Watts. No competent critic of today would claim for Watts a leading place among
the artists, and maybe they are right who maintain that in his
deeply mystical representations of reality he sold his artistic
birthright for a pot of message! Too patently didactic, his paintings are not truly great art. Yet, for all that and perhaps for that
very reason, they may be all the more homiletically helpful. One
of his best-known pictures is called "Great Possessions." It depicts the back of the rich young ruler as, at the crucial moment
of his life, he turns away from Christ. While still working on
the canvas in his studio, Watts remarked to a friend: "I am doing

95

a man's back to explain the text: 'He went away sorrowful, for he had great possessions.' Fancy a man turning his back on Christ rather than give up his goods! They say his back looks sorry: that is what I meant it to express."

Or examine another famous painting. A prized possession of the Wolverhampton Art Gallery, it was executed by Sir John Collier and is entitled "Sentenced to Death." The scene depicted is a doctor's consulting room. In the foreground we get a rear view of the physician, who sits fingering his stethoscope and facing the young man who has come to him for examination. On the pale features of the patient the artist has portrayed the marks of tuberculosis, and the somewhat melodramatic caption discloses the medical verdict. The young man is listening to his fate. No preacher can contemplate that painting without being deeply touched and having his creative faculty stirred and stimulated. Whenever afterward, in his study of the New Testament, he stumbles on these awful words "condemned already" (John 3:18), the scene delineated in that haunting picture will be floodlit in his recollection.

Or, again, examine—as the last of our trilogy—a magnificent modern painting which for Douglas Webster flashes with spiritual meaning. This is how he turns it into a coruscating illustration for a discourse on the Cross:

One of the most remarkable paintings of our generation is Salvador Dali's "Christ of St. John of the Cross" which hangs in the Glasgow Art Gallery. Immediately one recognizes in this treatment of the Crucifixion something different from the older, more familiar, presentations. The Cross itself is massive; it looms over the world. The figure on the Cross is young and strong; He is "the young Prince of Glory" as in the original version of Isaac Watts' famous hymn. He seems to be holding back the great volume of darkness, forcing its retreat. In the foreground earth and sea and sky are lit with a new light streaming from the Crucified. But the Cross remains, dominating the world, and the world the artist sees is the world on which Christ looks from the Cross. And how different it looks in that perspective! [6]

What an inspiring painting from which to sketch a pen-picture for inclusion in a sermon on Gal. 6:14: "But God forbid that I should glory, save in the cross of our Lord Jesus Christ, by whom the world is crucified unto me, and I unto the world"!

Closely adjacent to the field we have just surveyed is that of sculpture. Great sculpture is a sort of solid scripture.

In this realm I have been struck by three remarkable examples, each luminously expressive of some profound religious truth.

One is to be found in Sweden, a powerful group of statuary standing in front of the Stockholm Museum. It is named "The Belt Wrestlers," and it shows two men, two vigorous and athletic figures, locked together in a sinewy grapple. They are enclosed within a single band, and each holds in his right hand a naked knife. The band is too strong for them to break, so there is no chance of their getting away from each other, and each is resolved that his fellow shall die. No truce can be concluded between them. It is to be a fight to the finish. There indeed is a sermon in stone. We should have to go far to find its equal. As an illustration for a discourse on that internal strife of which Paul speaks in Gal. 5:17—"For the flesh lusteth against the Spirit, and the Spirit against the flesh: and these are contrary the one to the other: so that ye cannot do the things that ye would"—it is surely without peer.

Another sermon-picture from the sphere of sculpture may be seen in the porch of the art gallery in Sydney, Australia. It is done in bronze, the work of Andreoni. Its title is "The Pharisee," and embossed in Hebrew on its base are the words: "He that is without sin among you let him first cast a stone" (John 8:7). With the skill of genius, the sculptor has contrived to represent on the statue resolution tempered by reflection. In the figure's

[6] *In Debt to Christ* (London: The Highway Press; Philadelphia: Fortress Press, 1957), p. 9.

97

right hand is a jagged stone, and his body is poised, like a javelin in the grasp of a mighty thrower, ready to hurl the missile at the adulteress; but on the metal face there is a twist of moral pain. He has remembered.

Yet another illustration of this type may be discovered in Copenhagen. It is surely one of the most moving pieces of monumental masonry in the world. Here is how I have actually spoken of it in a sermon:

Not long ago I was in the Danish capital and, whilst there, visited the famous Glyptotaket, in which some of the finest statuary in existence is on exhibition. Among the objects of art I saw was a group of sculptured figures in white marble, the work of Rodin, the French master. It is called "The First Funeral," and it depicts Adam and Eve bearing to burial the body of the murdered Abel. To an almost startling extent the sculptor has succeeded in reproducing in stone the emotions of the primal pair as they carry the corpse to the grave. Eve is distracted with grief; Adam, less sensitive and more restrained, looks down in sorrow and bewilderment at the cold, limp form in his arms. No one gazing on that group of statuary can fail to be impressed with the fact and awful mystery of death.

There is still another field in which we may search for stirring and stimulating illustrations—newspapers and magazines.

We will begin with the newspaper. In some quarters there is a deplorable tendency to look down the nose at the press. It is a species of intellectual snobbery, and like all snobbery it tends to underestimate the thing it despises. For, whether judged from the standpoint of literary quality—I speak, of course, only of the better type of newspaper—or from that of the phenomenal quantity of its output, the press must surely take a foremost place among the marvels of the modern scene.

Someone has happily christened the newspaper "the history of the world today," a history chronicled almost as soon as it happens. Would it not be oddly inconsistent to affect an absorbed interest in the writings of Gibbon, Macaulay, Trevelyan, Bryant,

98

but to show no interest whatever, certainly no appreciative interest, in the writings of the journalists who are the historians of the present hour? Considering the haste with which their history has to be recorded, the standard of journalism in general is astoundingly high.

Or reflect on the quantity of matter which, like a river in spate, is ceaselessly pouring through the printing machines. George Saintsbury has an illuminating comment on this subject.

It is a commonplace that an ordinary daily newspaper contains the matter of a fair-sized octavo volume, and an ordinary weekly newspaper contains about the same, or a little less. So that, if a man reads only one of each, he reads an octavo volume every day throughout the year, or about ten thousand in thirty years, quite independently of all other reading.

A wise preacher will not waste his precious time with the gutter press, but neither will he overlook the fact that there are noble newspapers absolutely teeming with potential word-paintings for insertion in his pulpit work. John Wesley, as is well known, said that he consulted his paper to see what God was doing in the world, and Newman Hall insisted that a minister should read two things—the Bible and the London Times.

In the days of Christ there was, it appears, a very crude precursor of the modern newspaper called "Acta Diurna." There is no indication that Jesus ever saw a copy of it; but he certainly did evince a sense of the homiletic value of passing events, as we know from his public reference to the fall of the Tower of Siloam and to the fate of the Galileans whose blood Pilate had mingled with that of their sacrifices (Luke 13:1-5).

For us ministers of the Word to ignore the possible illustrative contribution of the newspaper to our sermons is to involve ourselves and our work in a serious impoverishment. There are many word-pictures in the papers, and in this connection J. A. Kern offers some admirable advice: "Take up the first newspaper that comes to hand and see how many illustrations of spiritual truth it furnishes." Capital counsel which no sensible preacher will contemn.

The following are two samples from my personal collection. This, for instance:

I clipped from the newspaper the other day a paragraph in which a great German surgeon described a dangerous operation he had performed on a human heart. Opening the patient's thorax, he found that the heart was encased by a wall of stone. This wall was gradually thickening and hardening, and would at last have altogether prevented from functioning the delicate organ it enclosed. The surgeon's task was no easy one. It was to break up that stony encasement and take it away bit by bit without injuring the heart—an undertaking calling for coolness and skill of no common order. After a fatiguing effort, the thing was done. The cement-like casing was removed, the patient recovered rapidly and was soon back at work.

Does not that present us with a graphic picture for a discourse on Ezek. 36:26: "A new heart also will I give you, and a new spirit will I put within you: and I will take away the stony heart out of your flesh, and I will give you a heart of flesh"?

Or this. Picking up the newspaper one day I came upon an article on poultry. Now, poultry has not the slightest interest for me, or perhaps it would be truer to say that the interest poultry possesses for me is purely post mortem! I wondered, therefore, afterward why I had bothered to read the article at all; yet, whatever the reason, I did so, for I felt that there was something in it for me. There was. Later in a sermon on Isa. 40:31, "They shall mount up with wings as eagles," a sermon to which I gave the title "The Price of the Pinionless Life," I illustratively employed the following excerpt from the press, snipped from that article on poultry. Here is what I said:

Recently I read in the newspaper about a novel experiment made not long since in the United States. It was an attempt to produce a wingless fowl. The theory was that if the fowl was not furnished

100

with wings its body would be plumper in places where the flesh was more palatable. By clever crossbreeding and other highly technical processes on which I am not competent to comment, the feat was at last performed. The monstrosity was produced. The pinionless poultry was hatched. But the thing was not a success. It was found that the carcasses of the wingless fowls were, on the whole, smaller and not larger, as had been hoped, than those of the normal breeds, and the eggs of the females fewer in number and less in size and weight. So the ingenious experiment proved abortive and was abandoned, and the experimenters were glad to revert to the normal methods of breeding.

Turn now to magazines. Here, too, there is a positively inexplorable wealth of fresh pictorial potential. Take a case in point. Some time ago a popular journal printed the following intriguing story, a story admirably adapted to form a front-rank sermon illustration. A lady tells of a visit to a famous Harley Street heart specialist:

When I went to see him, he asked me to lift a bronze statue; I did—with an effort. And after I had subsided with it he said: "It weighs sixteen pounds—think of carrying that around, upstairs and everywhere you go! It's not surprising that your heart and respirations soon began to feel the strain."

Where could we find a more perfect pen-painting for an address on Heb. 12:1: "Let us lay aside every weight"?

Another spacious field in which we may hunt for sermon illustrations is history. What a panoramic expanse confronts us here with many an exquisite and exciting word-picture for our sermons!

So many brilliantly illuminative examples will come thronging to everybody's mind that there is no need to multiply instances.

Let two suffice.

Here is the first:

There is a stirring story, dating from the dawn of British history, which describes how, when William, Duke of Normandy, landed

THE ART OF ILLUSTRATING SERMONS

in 1066 at Pevensey on the Sussex coast, a trifling mishap befell him which was very differently interpreted by the intrepid warrior himself and by his credulous and vacillating followers. Leaping ashore from the ship, he missed his footing and fell full-length on the beach, clutching instinctively at the sand with both hands. "An evil omen!" cried his superstitious men. "No," countered the redoubtable conqueror, "I have taken possession of this land with my two hands. All that is here is ours!"

We can see at a glance how such a dramatic narrative might be pressed into service in a sermon on I Cor. 3:21: "All things are yours."

And here is the second historical illustration:

Few royal figures, surely, have crammed so much into so short a life-span as King Edward VI of England, son of King Henry VIII. Born in 1537, he died in 1553, not quite sixteen. Certainly he must be one of the very few boys of whom a full-scale biography has been written! At nine years of age, on the occasion of his accession to the throne, he made history. On February 20, 1547, after the ceremony in Westminster Abbey at which Archbishop Cranmer presided, the boy king was walking in procession toward Westminster Hall, where a banquet had been prepared. Just in front of him were officers of state bearing aloft three great swords. He asked what this meant, and they told him that the swords stood respectively for each of the three kingdoms united under his crown. "One is wanting," he exclaimed, "the Bible, the sword of the Spirit!" And he ordered that the large pulpit Bible should be taken from the lectern in the Abbey and carried with solemn dignity ahead of the symbols of worldly power. Thus it comes about that to this day the presentation to the sovereign of a copy of the Word of God is part of the English coronation service.

Besides those just mentioned, there is yet a further boundless territory in which illustrations may be tracked down—biography. Dr. Johnson spoke for many of us when he confessed that biography was the branch of literature which he liked best. Other

102

types of books—fiction only excepted, which is after all very largely merely disguised biography—exercise a limited and specialized appeal. Gripping some, they fail altogether to lay a hand on others. But biography has something for us all. He who is tired of "lives" is tired of life. Edmund Bentley has a whimsical stanza in his *Biography for Beginners* which runs as follows:

> The art of Biography
> Is different from Geography
> Geography is about maps,
> But Biography is about chaps.[7]

Maps are magnetic to some sorts of mind, and they are of obvious value to anyone contemplating a journey through an unknown land; but chaps possess a universal and unfailing fascination. In biography we are bound to come upon literally thousands of word-pictures for our sermons.

How much we may learn about any age simply by studying the life stories of its six most prominent men! Was it not Thomas Carlyle who contended that the history of any generation is the biography of its outstanding personalities?

To read the lives of, say, Winston Churchill, Franklin D. Roosevelt, Mahatma Gandhi, Nikita Kruschev, and John Logie Baird—would not that be a liberal education to anyone anxious to assess the character of the current age?

Autobiography is biography at its best. We recollect the aphorism: "An autobiography is what a biography ought to be"—and we agree with it! It is obvious that in honest autobiography the reader is sure to get closer to the heart of the subject than in any study, however intimate and candid, from the pen of a mere observer. No man is in a better position to write his life story than himself; in a sense, nobody else can write it—all such attempts are mere approximations. From Augustine's *Confessions* to those of Rousseau, from Bunyan's

[7] (London: The Bodley Head, 1910).

103

Grace Abounding to Samuel Pepys' *Diary*, there is no biography like autobiography.

And yet what lifelike delineations of their subjects the classic biographers have given us! Who can think of Johnson without his Boswell, of Scott without his Lockhart, of Gladstone without his Morley? These monumental biographies make immortal the men who wrote them as well as the men about whom they were written; and, incidentally, they provide the preacher with a wealth of human data with which to garnish his discourses.

Take three samples.

First this from one of the most disturbing autobiographies of modern times. It is a deeply moving narrative which we may employ antithetically as an introduction to a sermon on the cross of Christ. We might word the illustration like this:

In that very challenging book, Vera Brittain's *Testament of Youth*, there is a passage of almost unbearable poignancy in which she describes how, some years after the death of her brother, who was killed during World War I in the fighting among the hills of northern Italy, the Imperial War Graves Commission decided to replace with a stone monument the plain wooden cross which had stood at the head of his last resting-place. The family begged to have the cross sent home; and, when it arrived, it proved a grim and gruesome object, stirring sickening memories. Yet, for all that, the Brittains were glad to have it, because, as Vera explained: "It's a strange world where the symbols of people count for so much more because they are all one has left!"

Thank God, the cross is not all we have left of Jesus! Not only has he survived it, he has triumphed over it, and now: "Christ being raised from the dead dieth no more" (Rom. 6:9).

Next take this moving illustration from the recently issued memoirs of a distinguished Scottish minister. In his brilliantly written autobiography, *The Glimmering Landscape*, Charles L. Warr gives an impressive example of the extraordinary literary power of the Bible. He records an incident in the life of Sir James Irvine, principal of St. Andrews University.

One Sunday, when reading the New Testament lesson in the University chapel, something queer began to happen. The passage was that descriptive of our Lord healing a man who had been blind from birth. All of a sudden, Irvine found himself no longer in the chapel. He was standing among the crowd on a dusty roadside witnessing Christ's act of healing. He felt on his head the strong Syrian sun, and in his nostrils was the smell of the hard-baked ground and of the sweating people, pressed close together. He saw Christ's every movement, watched fascinated as He placed the dust mingled with spittle upon the blind man's eyes, heard Christ tell him to go and wash in the Pool of Siloam . . . Then he found himself standing once more at the lectern, concluding the passage from which he had just been reading. Shaken, and perspiring profusely, he returned to his stall.[8]

That is a striking, not to say startling, instance of the impact which the Word of God can make on an imaginative and impressionable mind. We may use the illustration sometime in connection with a sermon on Heb. 4:12: "The Word of God is living and powerful."

On the same topic, but drawn from a widely different life story, is our third biographical illustration. It is an excerpt from Roy MacGregor Hastie's The Life and Times of Nikita Kruschev, and it brings into focus the fact that it is tragically possible to be quite at home with the text of the Bible and even, with the aid of a phenomenal memory, to be able to reel it off by the yard in a public assembly, and yet to be utterly unaffected by its moral challenge and an alien to its transforming potency. Relating how as a boy in the Don Valley of the Ukraine, he came in 1903 under the influence of Christian teaching, attending confirma-

* The Glimmering Landscape (London: Hodder & Stoughton, 1960), pp. 203-204. Used by permission of C. L. Warr and Hodder & Stoughton.

tion classes, and flirting with the catechism, Kruschev himself has this to say: "I used to go every Sunday to the priest's house to learn how to be a good Christian. When we did well we got sweets and tea to take home. Once I got a prize for learning the Four Gospels by heart and reciting them nonstop in church." There, surely, is a memorable word-picture, culled from a surprising quarter, emphasizing the indispensability of faith as an ingredient in Bible study and the utter moral futility of such study without it. The narrative reminds us of Heb. 4:2: "The word preached did not profit them, not being mixed with faith in them that heard it."

Poetry is another realm of gold in which we may track down illustrations for our discourses. Not all poetry, of course! Much modern verse, with its harlequin imagery and experimental rhymes and rhythms, not to mention its doubtful intelligibility, will be of no use to us whatever. There are, however, thank God, some present-day poets who do not specialize in verbal vermicelli, and in their published works we can find luminous passages which may contribute to our pictorial purposes.

Look at three instances.

One is by Christopher Morley. It is part of a lyric inspired by —of all things—a telephone directory. A telephone directory hardly seems the sort of literature to make a man wax lyrical. Yet that was the effect it had on Christopher Morley. To his fecund fancy it suggested the possibility of conveying to the whole of mankind some acceptable message. The last verse of the poem runs:

> A million hearts here wait our call,
> All naked to our distant speech:
> I wish that I could ring them all
> And have some welcome news for each.[9]

[9] From *Chimneysmoke* by Christopher Morley. Copyright 1921, 1949 by Christopher Morley. Published by J. B. Lippincott Company.

Had Morley but realized it, he might have found in the Christian gospel the very news he was seeking, news for everybody, news to make all men glad.

Another unforgettable example crops up in the writings of W. H. Auden. Few analyses of the psychology of modern youth excel or exceed this one in piercing penetration:

> To be young means
> To be all on edge, to be held waiting in
> A packed lounge for a personal call
> From long distance, for the low voice
> That defines one's future.[10]

That description of the teen-age mentality of our time displays sympathetic insight and understanding, and shows how vulnerable young people can be to the evangelistic challenge.

The third poetic sample is selected from the works of John Betjeman. Entitled "Before the Anaesthetic," it purports to be the thoughts of a man, a conventional and nominal Christian, to whom his faith has been no more than a comfortable illusion, but who suddenly finds himself in a hospital awaiting a major operation. Lying in bed, he hears the peal of the bells in the nearby church of St. Giles, which he had been in the habit of attending; and all at once he becomes almost panic-stricken as he realizes that the Christ he has hitherto worshiped is not the true Christ: urgently, desperately, as he faces this physical ordeal, he feels the need of the true Christ. With the sure touch of a master, the poet puts these words into his mouth:

> Illuminated missals—spires—
> Wide screens and decorated quires—
> All these I loved, and on my knees
> I thanked myself for knowing these
> And watched the morning sunlight pass
> Through richly stained Victorian glass

---

[10] *The Age of Anxiety* (New York: Random House, 1948), p. 43.

And in the colour-shafted air
I, kneeling, thought the Lord was there.
Now, lying in the gathering mist,
I know that Lord does not exist;
Now, lest this "I" should cease to be,
Come, real Lord, come quick to me.[11]

What a bright, illuminating window such an illustration might be in a discourse on John 4:24: "God is a Spirit: and they that worship him must worship him in spirit and in truth"!

Still pursuing our search for sermon-paintings, we come to yet another prairie-like expanse—fiction.

Proverbially, truth is stranger than fiction; homiletically, it is also stronger than fiction. Still, fiction does offer a wide range of possibility in the matter of pictorial potential for preaching. Though not true to fact—to employ again the familiar distinction—great fiction is always true to life, and as such it is by no means to be despised as a domain in which may be prosecuted the quest for illustrative sermon materials.

The field of exploration here is horizonless. We have space for only two specimens, the first from a short story and the second from a full-length novel.

One of the most famous short stories in the world is "The Necklace" by Guy de Maupassant, the brilliant French writer, whose life is itself a tragic commentary on the truth of the text: "The way of transgressors is hard" (Prov. 13:15). The following is a summary of the tale:

The young wife of a government clerk is invited with her husband to the minister's ball. With much care and thought her costume is arranged, but it lacks jewels. Eager to shine as brilliantly as the rest, she asks to borrow from a rich friend, who opens her jewel-box and bids her choose. With trembling fingers, she picks out a diamond necklace and fastens it about her throat. The ball is entrancing. She is the cynosure of every eye. The minister himself smiles at the lovely lady in the necklace. At four in the morning she leaves the glittering scene. In a shabby taxi, she and her husband seek out their dingy dwelling. Before a mirror she removes her wraps to see herself once more in all her glory. Then, with a startled cry, she gasps, "The necklace is gone!" Feverishly, they search high and low for it, but without success. And at last they decide to buy one in its place and return it to the lender. In a fashionable jeweller's establishment they find one exactly resembling the one that was lost. Its price, they learn, is thirty-six thousand francs—a colossal sum for a government clerk! Borrowing the money at a high rate of interest, they begin a ten-year struggle, working day and night until the whole amount is paid. By now the clerk's wife is old and worn. In the Champs-Élysées one day she runs into her rich friend. At first the friend fails to recognize her, but presently she exclaims: "My poor Mathilde, what has changed you so?" "Ah, I have had a hard life. Do you remember the necklace you lent me once?" "Yes." "Well, I lost it." "What do you mean? You brought it back." "I brought back another just like it, for which we have been ten years paying." Her friend, deeply moved, took both her hands in hers as she cried: "But, my poor Mathilde, *my necklace was paste.*"

Verily, "what shadows we are and what shadows we pursue!" Paneled into preaching based on Matt. 16:26, "What is a man profited, if he shall gain the whole world, and lose his own soul? or what shall a man give in exchange for his soul?" that illustration can scarcely fail to prove singularly searching and challenging.

For our second story of this type we turn to fascinating fiction by A. G. Street titled *Farmer's Glory.* The pen-picture is a rhapsody on plowing, which, so far as my experience goes, is unique in literature. It gives us an altogether new slant on Luke 9:62: "No man, having put his hand to the plough, and looking back, is fit for the kingdom of God." Here is the relevant quotation:

Ploughing is the king of jobs. In itself it is all-sufficing and soul-satisfying. You English townsfolk who sneer at Hodge plodding at the plough-tail, do not realize that he pities you, in that you cannot plough and have never known the joy of ploughing. "But how monotonous and boring it must be," you will say, and in the saying you will display your ignorance, for ploughing is the most charming disguise that work can wear. The plough is a perfect implement. The coulter cuts the upper side of the furrow slice; the share cuts the underside; and the turnfurrow or mould-board inverts the whole. Therefore, if you are a competent ploughman, you are performing a perfect operation, and since when has perfection been monotonous? When once you have acquired the knack of it, it goes with the effortless urge of a sailing boat. The plough, which looks so clumsy and uncouth, changes its character. In conjunction with your team of horses, it becomes a glorious galleon, which you steer proudly over the rolling fields like some mariner of old. It is no longer an ugly, awkward, inanimate thing, but a delicately flexible instrument, which responds to your slightest touch.[12]

That fresh angle on plowing causes us to revise our conceptions of it and invests the words of our text for us with hitherto unsuspected meaning.

In addition to all this there is still another department of literature in which arresting word-pictures for pulpit use are likely to be tracked down—the drama. To be sure, in evangelical circles the drama has often been morally suspect, and sometimes not without good reason. Paul Sangster, in his admirable biography of his father, discusses the older man's attitude to this question. "He tended to view drama," says the son, "from a Johnsonian view, doubting if it 'promotes any truth, either spiritual or moral.'"

Yet at his best the playwright is himself a pictorial preacher, even though he speaks with the lips of others and addresses people who, if they recognized him in this role, would hardly pay him the compliment of a hearing. Beyond doubt the dramatist can be a profound and acute commentator on the ethical issues of life.

[12] (London: Faber & Faber, 1932), pp. 62-63.

Is there, for instance, anywhere a more powerful and revealing depictment of the manner in which the risen Christ can disturb and challenge and change the members of a soiled and blasé social group, making them face up realistically to the truth about themselves and come to terms with reality, than Jerome K. Jerome's beautiful fantasy, *The Passing of the Third Floor Back?* Or is there a more telling and compelling sermon on the ultimate folly of worldliness, the inexpressible tragedy of a life spent in Vanity Fair, than Sir Arthur Pinero's *The Second Mrs. Tanqueray?* Or is there a subtler diagnosis of the moral maladies of modern men than that of T. S. Eliot in his famous play, *The Cocktail Party?* In it he describes a conversation between Celia Coplestone, a young woman who has been indulging in an illicit love affair but who has broken it off abruptly because her conscience has suddenly become uncomfortable about it, and a psychiatrist, Sir Henry Harcourt-Reilly, to whom she confesses the sense of loneliness and listlessness and lostness which has accompanied her moral awakening. She says:

> It's not the feeling of anything I've ever done,
> Which I might get away from, or of anything in me
> I could get rid of—but of emptiness, of failure
> Towards someone or something, outside of myself;
> And I feel I must . . . atone—is that the word? [13]

There you have a dramatic situation from which a door opens directly onto the great doctrine of atonement. The word "atonement" occurs once only in the King James Version of the Bible, and even there it is a mistranslation. But the thought runs like a crimson thread all the way through the New Testament. "Jesus Christ, by whom we have now received the atonement." (Rom. 5:11.) Celia Coplestone felt she wanted to atone. She never could. None of us ever can. Atonement is God's task, and he alone can accomplish it.

[13] T. S. Eliot, *The Cocktail Party.* (New York: Harcourt, Brace and Company; London: Faber & Faber, 1950.)

General observation, the wise and wide use of the faculty of perception and discernment in the world of men and things, is still a further source of sermon illustrations.

And, in this connection, have you noticed how deftly the great preachers pick up word-pictures, as it were, in the bygoing? Here is a handful of instances. Spurgeon has only to sit for a while near the quaint little church of Okewood in Surrey, noting that the graveyard surrounding it is spoked with paths coming from various directions but all converging at the porch of the church, one path leading uphill, another downhill, a third through a tangle of thicket, a fourth over lands tilled by the toil of men—and all at once for him the scene becomes symbolic, a picture of the diverse and devious ways by which men come to Christ, some from the depths of self-despair, some from the heights of pride, some through the baffling wilderness of doubt, some through a life of strenuous moral effort (this last typified by the cultivated soil), but all winning through at last to the same gracious goal. To the nimble mind of the great preacher, the whole thing becomes an illustration for a sermon on Mark 1:45, "They came to him from every quarter," and the title he gives to the finished discourse is "Gathering to the Center."

Alexander Maclaren has only to watch someone making a carbon copy of a letter, and it leads him to reflect on the imperishable impression being made by the lowliest life in the world unseen. He remarks:

You and I write our lives as one of these manifold writers which you use. A thin filmy sheet here, a bit of black paper below, but the writing goes through upon the next page; and, when the blackness which divides two worlds is swept away, there the history of each life written by ourselves remains legible in eternity.

John Henry Jowett has only to chat for a little with two old cottagers, living "not far from one of the stately homes of England," and he discovers in their simple answer to a very ordinary question a profound comment on the spiritual life. "Can you see the castle?" he asks. "Only in winter time," is the suggestive reply.

George Campbell Morgan has only to walk eastward along Queen Victoria Street in London, and to note in so doing that on his left he passes first the *Times* newspaper office and then the headquarters of the British and Foreign Bible Society, and his reflective mind immediately perceives in that purely fortuitous fact a parable of the manner in which life is meant to lead us from the temporal to the eternal.

It goes without saying, of course, that to track down sermon illustrations in this fertile fashion we need to cultivate the faculty of imaginative vigilance. Not much point in a blind man trying to catch a fox. To be successful in our search for word-pictures we have to train ourselves to be keenly observant and to meditate deeply on what we see and relate it to our lifework. One man will notice more in the course of a stroll down a single street than another will on a trip round the world. So we must keep our eyes wide open (someone has said that a preacher ought to have eyes like portholes), studying closely men and things, touching life at as many points as possible, watching people at their work, listening to what they say in common conversation, taking every chance we get of seeing anything exceptional or extraordinary. And always the prevailing mood of our minds must be that of what has been paradoxically called "an alert passivity." "A man's study," declared Henry Ward Beecher, "should be everywhere—in the house, in the street, in the fields and in the busy haunts of men." Like Wordsworth the preacher may have his library within four walls but his study out-of-doors.

Here are a few specimens of the sort of illustrations which can be collected in this way:

Through the good offices of a friend, I once had the privilege of looking over the world-famous radar observatory at Jodrell Bank in

113

Cheshire. What a marvelous place it is! Twelve miles (as the crow flies) away from Manchester, of whose University it forms a part, its huge, saucer-shaped, mobile reactor resembles a giant ear listening in to the stellar universe. Just as I was about to be conducted round the site by one of the officials, a doctor of science, he was called to the control room and detained there for some time. On reappearing, he was profuse in his apologies for keeping me waiting, adding, by way of explanation: "I have just been listening to the explosions of stars which burst three million years ago!" "In that case, doctor," I replied, "I can hardly blame you for holding me up for a few minutes!"

The point of the illustration is, of course, that those who are preoccupied with eternal issues need not be unduly perturbed about the paltry things of time. Only, this must not be pressed too far, lest the false inference be drawn that, if only a man dwell deeply enough in thought on the great matters of eternity, it does not much signify whether or not he duly and diligently discharges the duties and functions of ordinary life.

Equally instructive and inspiring to me was a visit paid to the celebrated Royal Doulton Pottery at Burslem, Staffordshire.

There I watched with fascinated interest every process—save one —by which the grey, dull, lumpish clay was transformed into the elegantly fashioned and gorgeously decorated china figures for which the firm is famous—"a triumph of ceramics." I saw the granulation, the weighing, the mixing with powdered shell or calcined bone, the cleansing, the demetalling by electromagnetism, the dehydration, the pressing, the cutting, the molding, the firing, the glazing, the refiring, the polishing—and to nearly everything I could discern a spiritual analogy. But there was one thing I did not see. I did not see the artists. Into their studio I was not permitted to go, perhaps because I might have disturbed them at their delicate work or maybe for fear that I might spy out some of the secrets of their craft. Anyhow, I did not see the artists. And, musing on the matter, it seemed to me that there might be a symbolic significance in that fact. In this vast pottery which we call a world, we are allowed to see a great deal—the clay, the wheel, the fire, and all the disciplines re-

114

quired to bring forth the divine Artificer's design. What we are not allowed to see is the Artificer himself. In his sublime humility he remains invisible, yet without him nothing worthwhile can ever be produced.

Is not that likely to prove a usable illustration? One might build it into a discourse on Jer. 18:2: "Arise, and go down to the potter's house," where, we remember, the prophet saw a vessel formed, deformed, and reformed. We are never able properly to preach on that narrative until we have actually been to a pottery and seen things for ourselves.

Likely to be of special interest to our listeners (provided we do not regale them too often with such reminiscences), are illustrations of this type recruited during travel in foreign parts. Word-pictures sketched in our journeyings abroad are sure more than most to attract and sustain the attention of our hearers.

Consider a couple from my own repertoire.

First this:

In the Melbourne Museum in Australia I saw a glass case containing gilded models of the large nuggets of gold found at various times in the Commonwealth. Of these the biggest was discovered at Moliagul near Dunolly in Victoria. Those who came upon it were John Deason and Richard Oates. Digging just below the surface of a bank of earth on February 5, 1869, they felt their spades strike metal. Feverishly picking up the nugget and wiping away the soil with which it was encrusted, they saw that it was a lump of solid gold, which afterwards was found to weigh 2,520 ounces troy. Its value is now assessed at £35,500. Yet there, within the glass case, stood the exhibit. No precautions were taken to protect it. No officials stood by to ensure that it was not stolen. Anyone, so minded, could have broken the glass and removed it without difficulty. Why was it thus left unguarded? Because it was only a counterfeit. It was merely a model. It wasn't the real thing, so nobody wanted it.

Does not that forcibly remind us of the passage in the Gospel where the Pharisees, observing with malicious envy the extraordinary success of the ministry of Jesus, exclaim in vexed frustration: "Perceive ye how ye prevail nothing? behold, the world is gone after him" (John 12:19). The Pharisees had only a counterfeit religion, nobody wanted it; Jesus had the real religion, and the people flocked to hear him.

And now consider the second illustration in this class:

I well remember that once, traveling from Naples to Pompeii and skirting Vesuvius, I noticed how rich the soil was on the slopes of that crater-crowned cone, and how luxuriant the vineyards and olive groves which patch, as it were, the fringe of its garment. That soil was once volcanic dust, the dust which on August 24, A.D. 79, mushroomed from the summit of the mountain, hung for a while like an atomic cloud in the sky, blotting out the sun and plunging everything into pitch darkness, to fall finally like hot snow on all around. Then it was volcanic dust; now it is fertile loam.

Is there not a lesson here? Do we not often find the fairest flowers and choicest fruits of Christian character in those whose lives have been overshadowed by tragedy or overwhelmed by misfortune?

Real life illustrations of this kind surround us on all hands when we travel in foreign parts. Describing a tour of Europe from which he had just returned, Charles Silvester Horne declared: "I feel as if I shall never lack for illustrations again, so rich a fund has accumulated during these months." If we are similarly observant and reflective in our gypsyings abroad, we too may acquire a comparable collection of appealing word-pictures for our sermons.

Nor must we leave out of our list of illustrative sources pastoral visitation. Needless to say, I am not suggesting that we ought to regard each of the members of our church as a potential clinical case study, or deliberately to encourage them to tell us stories about themselves, so that we may later retail them in the pulpit. That would be a breach of confidence, a mean betrayal of trust.

One is full of sympathy for the old Scots woman who was visited in her last illness by John McNeill, and who solemnly adjured him: "Dinna ye mak' an anecdote oot o' me efter I'm deid!" (Whereupon, of course, as Andrew Blackwood pawkily observes, McNeill proceeded to tell the story up and down the world!)

Always in our visitation our paramount aim must be to assist those on whom we call. Yet often, without letting anything leak out that should not, we may be able to use as pictorial material in our sermons something they casually let fall—a quaint bit of homely philosophy, a thumbnail character sketch, the description of an interesting incident, and so on. Incidentally, and frequently without their being aware of it at all, they may aid us quite amazingly in illuminating our addresses.

The two abstracts hereunder are taken from my own pastoral casebook.

For insertion in a sermon on Eph. 5:18, "Be filled with the Spirit," take the following:

Some years ago I had the sad duty of officiating with a colleague at the funeral of a young woman. She was only thirty-six when she died. The disease which struck her down at an early age was that mysterious malady, so baffling to medical research, variously known as infantile paralysis and poliomyelitis. The trouble attacked her in a most distressing manner. It affected her lungs. They almost died in her living body, the muscles controlling their action becoming atrophied. She wanted to breathe, but could not; and, towards the end, her sufferings were truly terrible. Rushed to a hospital, she was thrust into an iron lung in the hope of thus stimulating her respiratory organs. But in vain. When they put her into the instrument, she made frantic signs that she wanted to be taken out; and, when taken out, she indicated desperately that she wanted to be put in. And after a week of dreadful anguish and agony she passed away. Standing at her graveside on a green slope above the white cliffs, I was stunned and overwhelmed by the irony and pathos of it all. It was a glorious summer day. A fresh wind was blowing in from the south, a bracing breeze, laden

117

with life, pregnant with vitalizing properties. Yet there she lay, dead in the midst of it all, because her lungs refused their office.

What a vivid picture of the present plight and predicament of the church—moribund in the midst of abundant life because she will not breathe it in!

From the same fruitful source stems a further illustration. It might be conscripted for service in a sermon on "Assurance" and founded on these three texts: "full assurance of faith" (Heb. 10:22); "full assurance of understanding" (Col. 2:2); "full assurance of hope" (Heb. 6:11). The record in the casebook runs like this:

Several years ago I was asked to visit an old man with the picturesque name of Jack Frost. It was June, and I hardly expected to find anyone of that name in England just then outside of a refrigerator! Anyhow, I went. To get to his house I had to toil up a narrow, crooked, cobbled street, but on reaching the top I was rewarded with a magnificent view of a harbor. Finding his cottage, I knocked at the door and presently was admitted. The room into which I was ushered was neat and clean, if somewhat sparsely furnished, and on a chair in the middle of it sat the man I had come to see. I could have wept at sight of him. He was gravel blind; he was almost stone deaf; he had had his right arm amputated when upwards of eighty because infected with gangrene. Shouting into his ear through a speaking trumpet, they told him I was there, and for a time he talked to me as an old man will. Then it was suggested that perhaps he would like to sing. Sing! I wondered what he could find to sing about—in his prison of darkness, in his prison of silence, in his lonely prison of pain. Then all at once my reverie was broken into by a thin, quavery voice. He was singing. Jack Frost was singing! And this is what he sang:

Blessed assurance, Jesus is mine!
Oh, what a foretaste of glory divine!
Heir of salvation, purchase of God,

118

Born of His Spirit, washed in His blood.
This is my story, this is my song,
Praising my Savior all the day long.[14]

Coming away from that cottage, I felt that not one of the hundreds of volumes of Christian apologetics I had read had put the case for the religion of Jesus half so cogently and compellingly as did that song of old Jack Frost. A Christ who can make a man sing in such circumstances is a Christ well worthy of the love and loyalty of our hearts.

The last hunting ground in which the trail of sermon illustrations may be followed is that which lies nearest home—personal life.
Let me in closing this chapter recall two such experiences of my own.
This, for a start:

I recollect going once into the Belgian Embassy in London. Entering the building, I was suddenly accosted by a man, a total stranger, who came up to me and, without anything in the nature of preliminary, said: "Excuse me, sir, has anyone ever told you that you are uncommonly like the king of Spain?" "The king of Spain!" My first reaction was to question the man's sanity; my second was to feel sorry for the king of Spain! Anyhow, I pushed the remark into a pigeonhole in my mind and "forgot" all about it. A month or two later, however, I chanced to be in Scotland and, whilst there, invited a cousin of mine to lunch in a Glasgow restaurant. Sitting next to me at the table, she remarked quite casually: "I suppose you know that on your mother's side of the family you originally hailed from Spain!" "Spain!" I ejaculated. "I had no idea that we had sprung from Spain!" And then into my mind slipped the recollection of that odd observation in the Belgian Embassy not long before. He had told me that I was like the king of Spain, and now she was telling me that we had come from Spain. And all at once I began to see that there might be

[14] Fanny J. Crosby, "Blessed Assurance."

a vital link between the two facts. Perhaps I resembled the king because I belonged to his race; maybe I shared his likeness because I shared his life.

And is not that, after all, what this word means: "As many as received him, to them gave he power to become the sons of God" (John 1:12)? We must share his life if we would bear his likeness.

And now this:

In 1940 I bought an enthralling book. It was entitled *My Pilgrimage* and it was the autobiography of F. W. Boreham. Having read most of the writings of the distinguished essayist, I devoured with delight this record of his life. The narrative, written in Boreham's sprightly style, made the persons, places, and situations it described live in my imagination. Then in 1956-57 I had the opportunity of touring Australia and New Zealand, countries which formed the major part of the setting of the book. Wherever I went in these young lands, I made a point of seeing the places mentioned in the memoirs and, if possible, meeting people who had known Dr. Boreham personally. In this way I visited Mossgiel in New Zealand, Hobart in Tasmania, and Armadale in Victoria, Australia. The crowning moment came, however, when in his modest but beautiful bungalow in a suburb of Melbourne I met Dr. Boreham himself. On getting back to Britain, I read that book again. And now it was to me a new volume altogether. Perusing its pages, I could see not only in imagination but in memory many of the scenes and persons portrayed. Above all, I could hear in it from first to last the living accents of the author.

In my reading of the Bible it has been somewhat the same. Time was when I thumbed its pages and dipped into its contents without knowing anything of the experiences it describes and without having made the acquaintance of its divine Author. But a day came when I met the Author face to face, and ever since I have found the Bible a new book, a book invested for me with fresh meaning and commanding power.

That illustration I have woven into a sermon on our Lord's pathetic lament: "Search the scriptures; for in them ye think ye have eternal life: and they are they which testify of me. And ye will not come to me, that ye might have life" (John 5:39-40).

There, then, are numerous fields in which we may hopefully hunt for sermon illustrations. Not that we should always be *consciously* tracking down word-paintings in such spheres. We shall have other thoughts in mind, other things on hand. But, if we know our business as preachers, we shall always be *subconsciously* searching for sermon-pictures to illuminate our work, always seeking for stories to illustrate *the* Story.

4

Drawing Them Up

Having rapidly reviewed the uses, types, and sources of illustrations, we come now to consider the all-important topic of composition, the art of drawing them up.

A moment's reflection should suffice to show that in this regard word-pictures fall into three broad categories: (1) those derived from literature; (2) those drawn from life; and (3) those devised by the imagination.

Let us look at them one by one.

We begin with those derived from *literature*. Such illustrations are ready-made and employing them is a comparatively simple affair. All we have to do is somehow mark them in the books we read and later transcribe them into our sermons.

Perhaps this is as suitable a place as any at which to interpolate a few relevant comments on the subject of reading in general. It goes without saying that as preachers we ought to be voracious readers. To browse in the broad field of literature should be our unfeigned and unfailing delight. What a pure joy it is to be a booklover! Gibbon, the historian, declared that he would sooner have his love of books than the wealth of Golconda. And Macaulay maintained that, if pressed to the odious option, he would rather be a poor man in a garret with a passion for good literature, than a king in a palace without it.

Apart from distinctively theological works, there are some

gritty books—big, sinewy volumes that threaten to throw us as we wrestle with them—which we must read if we are to prevent our mental muscles from growing flabby. To such we who are particularly interested in the pictorial aspects of preaching may go "as a slave is scourged to his dungeon"; but go we must, and we may find to our surprise and delight that even such arid regions may yield a thin illustrative crop.

Naturally, however, it is in books that we read for pleasure and as a relief from sterner studies that we are likeliest to come upon the picture-plunder we are seeking. If we are wise, our choice of books will range over a wide area. It will include history, science, travel, adventure, romance, essays, and in fact any work that may seem to have something usable to offer. Even books which do not appear to have a serious purpose may for us have a serious purpose, and we may stumble upon treasure trove in the most unpromising places. Our delving minds may strike a nugget of gold where we never expected to discover anything of the sort.

Years ago the editor of a popular weekly invited his readers to send in brief notes under the heading "Books that Have Helped Me." Among the items submitted was the following: "My mother's cookbook and my father's checkbook!" We too may find assistance in the most severely utilitarian volumes.

With all our reading, nevertheless, we must be careful not to become "bookish," ministerial counterparts of the Gadarene maniac dwelling habitually among the tomes! When a well-known modern author issued his autobiography under the title *Ink in My Veins*, his publishers dispatched hundreds of postcards announcing its appearance: upon which the postal authorities, evidently apprehensive for the author's physical welfare, stamped in flaming scarlet: "Blood-donors urgently wanted!" Some of us preachers are desperately in need of the blood donor. We have on our faces the sallow look which comes of overmuch burning of the midnight oil—not always, by the way, the

123

oil of inspiration. A friend of mine who gave up a leading position as a business executive to become a Christian minister pointed in my presence one day to a preacher of this type, and said: "I wonder if *I'll* ever be like that!" Knowing him well, I dismissed the idea with a smile; yet for many of us this is a real peril and the moment we succumb to it we are done for, so far as being effective pictorial preachers is concerned. We should, then, read as widely as possible and always, as we read, we should keep a sharp lookout for illustrations which may be borrowed bodily from books and incorporated with due acknowledgment in our pulpit work.

Next we pass to the second class of sermon illustrations— those drawn indirectly from *life*. And here the first thing to be noted is the absolute necessity that we should train ourselves to be observant, to acquire the art of being "quick on the uptake" with reference to anything possessing illustrative interest, to be able in a flash to see a story in a situation or event, swiftly to perceive its plot and the exact application of its moral to some facet of truth or duty or experience. If we are thus vigilant, life will present us with countless vivid word-paintings with which to grace and to garnish our sermons.

A word now about the vital question of note-taking. One of our elementary requirements as preachers is a pocket-sized jotter of some kind, which may be used for sketching illustrations which come to us from life itself; and which we should always carry with us, together with pen or pencil, so that without delay we may block out any prospective sermon-pictures that come our way. Not only must we take note of them, we must take notes of them.

Illustrations, like babies, have a habit of being born at awkward times. We sit patiently in our studies for hours, or even pace the floor distractedly, vainly endeavoring, with Sunday looming ominously in the offing, to lay our fingers on some precise pen-painting we want. And then—frustrated, baffled, disappoint-

124

ed, almost in despair—we go out into the street or board a bus; and, lo, the birthpangs of an illustration are upon us!

What are we to do then? Provided we have had the foresight to furnish ourselves with handy notebooks, we are in no difficulty. Plucking the jotters from our pockets, we take pen in hand there and then, while the illustrative idea is still fresh and luminous and creative in our thoughts, and set down as much of it as we can. "In this world," wrote F. W. Robertson, "things can be felt but once: you cannot recall impressions. The lesson to be drawn from this is that, while the impression is strong, while the mood is on one, it is vital to get the thing down, lest it evaporate like mist on a May morning."

In line with this was the habit of Hobbes, the philosopher, of whom it is told that "he carried an inkhorn in the head of his walking-stick and would interrupt himself anywhere to put down anything that seemed to flash into his mind." Similar was the practice of John Wesley and Sir Walter Scott, each of whom had an inkpot at his saddlebow. Both would doubtless have subscribed to the dictum of Marcus Dods: "Don't despise a pen-and-ink memory!" "The horror of that moment," cries the King in Through the Looking Glass, "I shall never, never forget." "You will, though," corrects the Queen, "if you don't make a memorandum of it."

This passion for note-taking Emerson shared to the full. Of him it is recorded that whenever a thought struck him—though it might be in the middle of the night—he would immediately jot it down. His wife relates that once she was awakened during the hours of darkness by hearing him rummaging about in a drawer. "Anything wrong, Ralph?" she inquired sympathetically. "Have you got a pain?" "No, my dear," came the answer, "not a pain, only a thought!"

On the advisability of thus making an immediate memorandum of any illustration we come across, however inopportune the time or unconventional the place, the great preachers speak with

125

one voice. Typical of many others is the following testimony by Spurgeon:

Whenever I have been permitted a sufficient respite from my ministerial duties to enjoy a lengthened tour or even a short excursion, I have been in the habit of carrying with me a small notebook in which I have jotted down any illustrations which have suggested themselves to me by the way. My recreations have been all the more pleasant because I have made them subservient to my lifework. The notebook has been useful in my travels as a mental purse. If not fixed on paper, ideas are apt to vanish with the occasion which suggested them.

How much better to be prepared for the unpredictable illustrative inspiration than to run the risk to which A. J. Gossip confesses he sometimes exposed himself, by merely scribbling such notes on any scraps of paper he happened to have about him at the time. When tempted to do so, we ought to call to mind the case of the little girl who, when she had anything she specially wanted to remember, made a memorandum of it on both sides of a sheet of paper, convinced that if she lost the one she would always have the other. Never should we forget in this connection that if we put an "immortal" thought on a slip of paper, the paper may give us the slip and the "immortal" thought prove mortal enough. Pictorial ideas are far too precious to be placed thus in peril of perdition.

In his racy and very readable *Lectures to My Students*, Spurgeon—to quote him again—suggests that the "parchments" which Paul bade Timothy fetch from Troas to Rome may have contained notes of illustrations collected on his travels. Of that we cannot be certain. But, if we know our business, we shall carry with us in our peregrinations notebooks in which, without loss of time, we shall jot down accurate and detailed descriptions of the things that strike us as possessing possible value as pictorial material for our sermons, notebooks which will serve us in much the same manner as a sketchbook does an artist.

We come now to the third group into which illustrations may be broadly classified—those derived from the *imagination*. Some people, to be sure, would ruthlessly rule out of the sermon any word-picture not absolutely factual. They feel—and it is a true instinct which informs the feeling—that everything fictitious is utterly out of place in a discourse dealing with religious realities. But surely fiction is only objectionable in a sermon when it masquerades as fact and when therefore it represents a deliberate attempt to deceive. When that happens, the illustration is nothing more nor less than a lie, and the preacher who uses it knows it is a lie, and when he does use it he forfeits the chief source of his power—the inner reinforcement of the Holy Spirit—for the Holy Spirit cannot be party to the perpetration of a fraud. A loss of such gravity can never be compensated for by any alleged oratorical gains accruing from the practice, and sermon paintings of that type ought to be rigorously banned from the pulpit.

It is another matter altogether, however, when word-pictures minted by the imagination are honestly retailed as such and when no pretense is made that they are anything else. In such circumstances they constitute no offense whatsoever to the most sensitive conscience, and the minister who is master of the art of producing and presenting them has in his hands a valuable accessory to his preaching of the Word.

There, then, are the three major classes into which, from the point of view of composition, illustrations can be divided.

Now, as we have noted, all of these varied types of sermon-pictures do not need to be drawn up in the same way. Illustrations of the first type do not need to be drawn up at all. They are readymade and have simply to be transcribed. With the second and third types it is different. Where they are concerned, the illustrations have to be planned, blocked out, and set down in detail on paper, as a painting has to be gradually built up on canvas, brushstroke by brushstroke. "Ah," said a young artist to Ruskin as together they contemplated a magnificent picture in an art gallery, "if only I could put such a dream on canvas!" "Dream on canvas!" mockingly echoed the critic. "It will take ten thousand touches of the brush on the canvas to put your dream there!" Before we can use word-pictures belonging to the last two categories, we shall have to put many touches on the canvas.

How are we to set about it? Well, the colors with which we work are words, and the wider our vocabulary and the finer our artistry in the handling of language, the better our sermon-paintings are certain to be.

There are four steps we must take in our efforts to cultivate style in the construction of illustrations. First, we must get to know individual words with their delicate shades of meaning and subtly evocative suggestions; next, we must learn the craft of phrasing; then, we must study the structure of the sentence; and, finally, we must become masters of the method of building pictorial paragraphs. Let us take these steps each in turn.

For a start, we must get to know words—as many of the 300,-000 in our lovely English tongue as we can. We must increase our working vocabulary. Yes—but how? The naïve reply would be that of Mark Twain: "Read the dictionary!" Nor is the advice as fatuous as it seems. Many notable men of letters have done just that when serving their apprenticeship. Robert Browning, for instance, did it, wading patiently through the voluminous verbosity of Dr. Johnson's *Dictionary*. Ministers of Christ have done it too. Samuel Chadwick once told his students that he had "worked his way through Chambers' *Dictionary*, word for word, four times"; and the biographer of Bishop Quayle records that "he read the dictionary as eagerly as most of us read fiction."

Of course, a far better method of extending one's vocabulary is to browse freely and deeply in the works of the great authors. When we read them, we should do so with pencil and pad handy, and any word we find them using which is attractive but unfamiliar to us, we should note down at once, together with a brief memorandum of its usage, consult the dictionary at the earliest possible moment to make sure of its meaning; and then, when occasion serves, try to employ the expression ourselves in writing or in conversation. If we do this, we shall be surprised how, before long, the number of vivid words at our command will have increased appreciably.

Here, however, we run up against a question mark: What sort of words should we choose for inclusion in our illustrations? About such, four things may be said.

For one thing, they should be simple words. There are times, of course, when it is perfectly permissible, perhaps even desirable, to use polysyllables. When on a famous occasion Winston Churchill told a political opponent bluntly that he was guilty of "a terminological inexactitude" meaning "a lie," Churchill was not out of order because he made the remark where presumably everybody could understand it. But if he had employed the same language at an election meeting in a rural area where his audience consisted for the most part of countrymen, he would not only have shown exceedingly bad taste, but also that he did not know his business as a public speaker. We all remember Dr. Denney's trenchant dictum: "The man who shoots above the target does not thereby prove that he has superior ammunition. He simply proves that he is not an accurate shot." If we purpose to present our message pictorially, simple language is a prime necessity, for nowhere else in the sermon is clear comprehension of every word by the congregation so absolutely vital to success.

Almost without exception, the speakers who have reached the widest possible constituency employed the simplest, homeliest, and commonest expressions. Luther's habit in this regard is well known. Wesley declared: "I design plain speech for plain people." Whitefield described the language he adopted in addressing the multitudes who flocked to hear him as that of the marketplace.

129

Taking an instance nearer to our own day, we turn to the great wartime speeches of Winston Churchill. At once we are struck by the extraordinary simplicity of the phraseology. "Give us the tools and we will finish the job." All but one of the terms monosyllables! Everybody understood that. But suppose he had said as someone has paraphrastically parodied him—"Donate us the implements and we will finalize the assignment"—a sentence meaning roughly the same thing; who then would have known what he was driving at?

It is no accident or coincidence that the wisdom of the people has embodied itself in pithy proverbs mentally easy to pick up and retain. Consider this, for example: "Let sleeping dogs lie." These four simple words, counseling a wise caution, have lingered long in the memory of the race. It would not, of course, be difficult to express the same thought in larger language somewhat after this fashion: "Permit the somnolent members of the canine species to continue in a soporific condition." But for how long would that be likely to linger in anybody's mind?

One author has plausibly suggested that if certain persons much addicted to the use of long words had had the writing of Isaac Watts's well known line, "How doth the little busy bee," we might have had something like this: "How doth the diminutive industrious apoidea." Very likely. When we contrast the limpid lucidity of Jane Taylor's haunting stanza, "The Star,"

> Twinkle, twinkle little star,
> How I wonder what you are!
> Up above the world so high,
> Like a diamond in the sky!

with the following polysyllabic parody:

> Scintillate, scintillate, globule vivific,
> Fain would I fathom thy nature specific;

130

Loftily poised in the ether capacious,
Strongly resembling a gem carbonaceous,[1]

we have no trouble in deciding which of the two types of terminology is the fitter for our illustrative needs.

John Oman, in *Concerning the Ministry*, relates that in 1786 a "refined" gentleman by the name of Harwood, offended by the stark simplicity and racy homeliness of the language of the King James Bible, undertook to rewrite it more elegantly. Here is his rendering of the reflections of the prodigal in the far country: "I am determined to go to my dear aged parent, and try to excite his tenderness and compassion for me—I will kneel before him and accost him in these penitent and pathetic terms: 'Best of parents! I acknowledge myself an ungrateful creature to heaven and to you!'" And the proposed translation of the parable ends thus: "Condescend to hire me into your family in the capacity of the meanest slave."

Anyone who thinks *that* an improvement on the older version must be singularly lacking in literary sensibility.

Our words must be simple. This is the first thing. There are, of course, two kinds of simplicity—that of the man who is simple because he cannot be anything else, and that of him who deliberately elects to be simple so as to accommodate himself to the most limited intelligence among his listeners. It is this second sort of simplicity which we must make it our ambition to achieve.

Curious, is it not, how inhibited and artificial some of us become the moment we put pen to paper? In ordinary speech we use simple, homely, familiar words forcibly and well; but as soon as we sit down to write, we cease altogether to be natural —start to walk, as it were, on verbal stilts—and affect a ponderous, pompous, cumbersome style which, in George A. Buttrick's expressive phrase, "lumbers along like a procession of elephants." We might as well try to paint a picture with molten tar as at-

---

[1] Quoted by George Henderson in *Lectures to Young Preachers* (Edinburgh: McCall Barbour, 1961), p. 78.

tempt to tell a story effectively in such a style. Montaigne would have it that we ought to write as we speak, composing as we talk in common conversation. To every form of literary composition that counsel might not apply, but to that of sermon illustrations it most emphatically does.

There is an instructive tale about a once-famous professor of divinity, Dr. E. Griffin. After hearing one of his students read from a sermon he had just written a passage of grandiloquent prose, Dr. Griffin stopped him and asked: "What do you mean by this paragraph?" The student told him in plain, direct, straightforward speech. "Now, then," said the professor, "sit down and write that."

When painting our word-pictures we would do well to emulate the excellent practice of Thomas Guthrie, who, before setting anything down in manuscript, would speak it aloud in his study. He did this because he realized that he was writing prose to be heard, not read; addressed to the ear, not the eye. Quite probably that was one reason why he became so extraordinarily successful as a pictorial preacher. Our words must be simple.

For another thing, they should be picturesque. On this topic I have touched already at some length, and so need not now linger long over it. It ought to be obvious that if we are to preach to any purpose pictorially the proper language for us to use is picture language—language which is richly adjectival, language which glows and burns like a stained-glass window. Raphael could never have painted his magnificent frescoes if the only pigments at his disposal had been blacks and browns and greys. To accomplish the desired results he had to have recourse to gorgeous purples, blazing yellows, cool greens, and brilliant vermilions. So in preaching. Drab, dull, lackluster words are worthless for the pictorial presentment of divine truth. We cannot paint verbal pictures with colorless language any more than Tintoretto could have painted his masterpieces with pitch. Our words must be picturesque.

For yet another thing, they should be modern. To speak tellingly to our contemporaries we shall have to talk the language of our time. The words we use may be old, but there must not be about them that mothball aroma of archaism which is fatal to effect in the world today. Spurgeon was a splendid pulpit orator in the England of the Victorian era—some would claim the greatest preacher who ever employed the English tongue—but Spurgeon's spacious oratory is as much out of date nowadays as the furniture of his period. We must address our age in its own idiom if we are to get our message over. Our words must be modern.

For a final thing, they should be congruous. The terms employed in the illustration must be in keeping with the character of the illustration itself. What point would there be in trying to sketch an etching on canvas or to use oils in the production of a watercolor? Each art form has its own implements and its own materials. So with sermon illustrations. The style must, as far as possible, be consonant with the nature of the word-picture. To be effective some stories must be told in homely language; others, in more ornate, elaborate phraseology, consistent of course with the personality of the preacher and with the congregation's powers of comprehension. Of Thomas Jefferson's style it was strikingly said that "it fitted the thought as the skin fits the flesh." That is style at its best—style utterly congruous with its theme.

All the same, while recognizing the importance of individual words in the illustration, we must also realize that it is one thing to have a wide range of colors under one's hand and quite another to know how artistically to apply them. The painter can do nothing without his pigments; but equally the pigments are only so many smears of colored chemicals on the palette until picked up and laid on the canvas by the touch of the master.

This brings us to the second step we may take toward the acquisition of an effective style for sermon illustration—that of learning the craft of *phrasing*. Syntax has more to do with

133

sense than we commonly suppose. Jonathan Swift defined style as "proper words in their proper places," but that's just the rub —to find the proper places for the proper words. On this subject John Bennett has the following arresting and illuminating sentences: "It would be impossible to convey any meaning if words were used in an isolated way. It is nonsense to say: 'Water of fetch pail a Jack went hill the up to'; but the meaning is quite clear when the order of the words is rearranged and the expression becomes: 'Jack went up the hill to fetch a pail of water.'" Oratorically speaking, a phrase consists of the number of words which can be comfortably uttered with one breath. The phrase can be defined as simply as that; and yet what almost limitless possibilities there are in the marshaling and manipulation of the terms of which it is composed, and how much there is to know about the framing of it which can never be learned by rule but only by steeping oneself in the style of the best authors.

The third step we must take in seeking to acquire a usable style for pictorial preaching is to study the structure of the *sentence*. In good writing the length of sentences varies greatly. Some are short, sharp, telegrammic; others are long, complex, compound. Where sermon illustrations are concerned, this variety in the length of the sentence is eminently desirable, for by means of it thought and feeling can keep pace with one another during the unfolding of the narrative. Brief, bullet-like sentences quicken the tempo when that is called for; the more leisurely and extended sentence is useful for descriptive passages. In any case, the really vital thing is to think of the sentence in relation to the listener's ability thoroughly to grasp its meaning at one hearing. The psychologists put it well when they say that the sentence ought to correspond to a single pulse of attention. No sentence should be so tediously extended that the congregation loses interest in it before it comes to a close; for, if they do, they lose interest not in the sentence only, but in the illustration as a whole. Strong, epigrammatic sentences, with the stress falling

134

either at the beginning or at the end, are best; sentences which pack truth in capsule form and make it easy to swallow at one gulp.

The fourth step is to tackle the building of the pictorial paragraph itself. This is a matter we must examine extensively: but, before addressing ourselves to it, there are five preliminary exercises in which it would be profitable for us to engage.

One is to read the autobiographies of professional storytellers, or books in which they discuss the principles and practice of their craft. Many exploratory errors we may spare ourselves if we take pains to benefit by their experience. From them we may glean many helpful hints about the conception, construction, and composition of sermon illustrations. We are not interested in the techniques of novel writing as such. Our concern is with something much simpler. Yet what they say about the short story in particular and literary art in general is directly relevant to our special field of study. Such masters of the craft as Flaubert, de Maupassant, E. Phillips Oppenheim, and O. Henry, have much to teach us about the production of word-pictures; and we can hardly fail to find stimulus and guidance in such a book as *The Basic Formulas of Fiction*, by William Foster-Harris.

The second exercise is to listen to as many as possible of the leading preachers of our time, particularly to those noted for their facility, fertility, and felicity in illustration. One of the most impoverishing features of the Christian ministry is the fact that, from the very nature of the case, we ministers seldom have the good fortune of hearing one another preach; and unhappily we do not always avail ourselves of such opportunities of the kind as do come our way, perhaps because we feel that it is wise to spend what scant leisure we have in some form of recreation which provides a complete break from the endless round and routine of our work. That is a temptation we must train ourselves to resist whenever we get the chance of joining the congregation of some outstanding pictorial preacher. There is no more expeditious method of learning how to illustrate sermons than by listening to those who can do it with the ease and finish of the expert.

The third exercise is to ferret for telling illustrations in the published discourses of popular preachers and to make an anthology of the finest of them. We can then try to break them down one by one, subjecting each to critical analysis as a botanist does a flower, noting on what lines it is constructed, how the several parts stand related to one another, and how they all conspire to create the intended impression. Doing this over and over again, we shall at last be able to tell at a glance how the plot of every sermon-story is built up and to what precise point it is that the whole illustration tapers like the blade of a sword. Thus we may learn the rudiments of our art from the acknowledged masters.

To this the fourth exercise is closely akin. It is to choose week by week from our collection of illustrations one of exceptional quality and get it, as we say, "off by heart," going over it again and again in our thoughts, alike with verbal accuracy and appropriate emotional accompaniments, and even, when occasion serves, reciting it aloud, until story, style, and structure are stamped upon our minds and the pattern of imagery forms a clear mental picture. This practice, if kept up, will aid us materially when making illustrations of our own.

The fifth and last exercise is a variant of the fourth. Only, in this case, instead of committing the word-picture to memory, we read it over many times and try to absorb as much of it as we can. Then, shutting the book, we endeavor to visualize the narrative in detail, asking ourselves what the plot was, what the description, characterization, dialogue, and what the point or moral. Afterward we write out the illustration in our own words, not so much attempting to reproduce the actual phraseology of the text as to portray the scene, situation, dramatis personae, and so on, without omitting anything vital to the understanding of the tale. On a really first-rate illustration we shall probably not be able to improve. Still, let us tell the story in our own style, and finally, opening the book again, compare our version with the original, looking for verbal variations, noting differences in the fashion in which the facts are organized and presented, and seeing how the two renderings vary in their modes of mounting to a climax and producing the desired effect. If we get into the habit of this, we shall find that after awhile our own versions are gradually approximating toward the excellence of the printed illustrations, and that the literary disparity between them is diminishing.

We have now reached a stage at which we are ready to start work on word-pictures of our own. How are we to set about it? Well, it may help us at the outset to get things into proper focus if we pause for a moment to remind ourselves that every story possessing strong human appeal contains three elements— plot, characters, and action.

"There are," wrote Robert Louis Stevenson, whose words on this subject ought to carry considerable weight, "three ways and three ways only, of writing a story. You may take a plot and fit characters to it, or you may take a character and choose incidents and situations to develop it, or lastly, you may take a certain atmosphere and get action and persons to express and realize it."

Whatever method we choose, we shall have when composing our word-pictures to adopt some such course as the following. First, we shall have to decide what truth or principle it is we desire to illustrate. Next we shall have to ask ourselves what story or incident can best serve our end. Then we must turn the story over and over in our minds until it becomes as real to us as if it had happened to ourselves or was actually taking place at that moment. After this we must settle on the angle from which it will be wisest to present the story, approaching it with a painter's regard for perspective. Now we can rough out the narrative in pencil on a pad, reading the draft again and again, touching it up here and pruning it there until it assumes as finished a form as we know how to give it. Then we may dictate it slowly into a tape recorder and afterward play it back as, with what detachment we can, we relax in an arm-

THE ART OF ILLUSTRATING SERMONS

chair and listen to it, several times if necessary. When we have brought it as close to perfection as possible, we can type it to our own dictation from the recording, sentence by sentence, arresting the machine at every full stop, and then lay the typescript aside for a few days until we can come to it again with freshly critical minds.

The placing of the parts of the illustration in proper sequence is of prime importance. An illustration should be shaped like a wedge, with everything narrowing to a point, and it is absolutely vital to ensure that the details of the narrative are so disposed as to bring things to a crisp, clinching close. As evidence of the difference the organization of the materials in a word-picture can make, consider these two handlings of the same anecdote. The first is by a gifted and scholarly writer who sets the incident down thus:

Mendelssohn one day went into a little village church and sat listening for a time to the organist as he sat playing. After a time he went up to him and asked to be allowed to play the organ. "I never allow anyone to play my organ," said the organist. The stranger persisted and he reluctantly yielded. Quietly the stranger took his place at the instrument and, as his hands moved gently over the keys, there burst from that little organ such strains of music as never before had filled that place of worship. The organist was spellbound, and when, on asking the stranger who he was, he learned that it was Mendelssohn, the organist said: "How could I have kept my organ from the great master-player?" [2]

That is a competent presentment of the narrative. The facts are given, the situation described, the point made. But are these things done to the best advantage? Is it politic, for example, to disclose to the hearer from the start who the mysterious stranger is, or would it not be wiser to keep that a secret till the

[2] A. Naismith, Notes, Quotes and Anecdotes (London: Pickering & Inglis, 1962), pp. 90-91.

end? The answer will at once suggest itself when we examine
W. E. Sangster's exquisite version of the same tale:

Most people have heard the moving story told years ago by the
organist of the great church at Fribourg. He was sitting, he said, on
his stool one day, playing his famous instrument. The church was
empty. As he played a stranger came in, listened for a while in the
aisle, and then came and stood behind his stool. For half-an-hour he
continued to watch and listen. Presently he spoke: "May I take the
instrument?" he said, and the organist refused. Still the stranger
waited. At intervals he repeated his request, and finally, without much
grace, the organist unwillingly gave way. The stranger took the stool,
and sat for a few moments looking at the keys. Then he began—
and immediately there burst forth from the eager pipes grander music
than that grand organ had ever yielded before. It filled the empty
church. It dwelt in every hollow of the branching roof. It wakened
sleeping choirs of angels. The stone pillars shouted aloud their praise.
Overcome, the organist seized the shoulders of the stranger from
behind and, as the melody died away, he said: "Who are you?"
"Mendelssohn!" said the stranger. "And to think," replied the organist, "that I nearly refused Mendelssohn the use of my instrument." [3]

There is no question as to which is the finer rendering.
Sangster has constructed his word-picture with a craftsman's
care. The incident happens in Fribourg; the church is empty;
the stranger listens for *half-an-hour*. Note, further, the vigor
and imaginative beauty of the description: eager pipes; the
branching roof; sleeping choirs of angels. Observe, too, the powerful action prompted by strong feeling overcoming conventional
restraints. The organist seizes the stranger from behind by the
shoulders. And, lastly, look at the wondering and wistful words
in which the organist sums it all up: "And to think that I nearly
refused Mendelssohn the use of my instrument!" Could any

[3] *Ten Statesmen and Jesus Christ* (London: Hodder & Stoughton, 1941), pp.
26-27.

sentence better bring out the whole point of the story? That is the sort of excellence at which we should aim in the execution of our sermon illustrations. We shall probably never attain it, but at least it will prove a challenging and inspiring ideal.

If we are inclined to grudge the time and labor involved, let us for our encouragement reflect that not even the masters of the art have been exempted from the most exacting toil. Consider, for instance, this enlightening confession by John Watson, better known as "Ian Maclaren." He is relating how he composed his short stories, and here is what he says:

Each one was turned over in my mind for months before I put pen to paper. It took a prodigious amount of labour before I even had a story formed in my head. Then I blocked it out at one sitting. Then the thing was put aside while I went over and over in my mind each detail, each line of the dialogue, each touch of description, determining on the proper place, attitude, shape, colour and quality of each bit, so that in the end the whole might be a unit and not a bundle of parts. By and by came the actual writing with the revision and correction which accompanies and follows. I was obliged to make slow progress.[4]

With such an example before us we ought not to be too disheartened if we feel that our development as sermon illustrators is not as swift as we had expected. For our comfort we ought to recall the story of the buoyant youth who, having taken a few lessons in a correspondence course in journalism, wrote gushingly to his tutor: "You have taught me to write with great facility." To which the tutor replied: "I hope to teach you to write with great difficulty!" Ben Jonson knew well what he was about when he declared: "Ready writing means not good writing, but good writing brings a ready writing." It is the verdict of experience that the labor gets lighter as we go on, and we may come at last to have something of the assured touch of the master

---

[4] William Robertson Nicoll, *Ian Maclaren* (London: Hodder & Stoughton), pp. 166-67.

artist. Practice makes not only for perfection but for facility. "The best way to learn how to illustrate," comments A. Lindsay Glegg, "is to start doing it." "Learn by doing" is the maxim. When a group of students went once to William Hunt, the painter, with a host of questions about the techniques of art, he brushed aside their eager interrogations with the cry: "Do! Do! Do! Let your picture go and do another!" That is capital counsel in connection with the craft of sermon illustrating.

In the process of literary composition three mental states can be clearly distinguished. The first is the contemplative, when the author is thinking out the details of his subject; the next is the creative, when he is actually engaged in the execution of it; and the third is the critical, when after a lapse of time he is revising and recasting what he has composed. After having polished our illustrations as finely as we can, we should put them away for awhile and then take them out again, working on them as an artist works on his canvases, touching up the colors, strengthening the outlines, adding brilliant vividness to the minute detail.

Thus we shall best draw them up.

5

Storing Them Away

Hoarding is a common habit. The ant has it, stuffing into a pocket in the earth its modest stock of grain. The squirrel has it, thriftily hiding in its nest its tiny store of nuts. The bee has it, husbanding in the waxen cells of its hive the yellow honey. And— to pass with one step from little things to great—in our preaching we ought to have it too, especially with regard to illustrations. "First stalk them, then stock them," should be our motto.

The reason the small creatures at which we have just glanced hoard supplies is obvious. They do so because, divinely gifted with instinctive prescience and prudence, they are wise enough in the luxuriant and plenteous summer to anticipate the needs of the lean and hungry winter.

Similar wisdom ought surely to characterize the ministers of the Word of God. To have sufficient pictorial materials to cover and to cope with current requirements is all very well, but always we should have something in reserve to meet the recurring demands of the future. J. Berg Esenwein put the matter mildly when he said: "Inspiration is not always on call." But, whether inspired or not, we have to preach, and we ought to preach as interestingly and instructively as we can. Like Oliver Twist, our congregations are always asking for more; and woe to us if, from time to time, we have nothing fresh to offer them.

For our admonition we preachers ought to hang in the picture galleries of our imaginations the scene Christ painted in his parable of the man at whose home a famished traveler arrived at midnight, when he had nothing to set before him; and we should let that meaningful episode underline for us the urgency and importance of storing, amongst other sermon substance, effective illustrative materials. Not only do we need a sufficiency for immediate requirements; we need a surplus for commitments in the years ahead. As James Black humorously expresses it: "You will have to see to it that your store is replenished as quickly as it is used. Otherwise there may be a new rendering of the ancient and pitiful tragedy of Mother Hubbard. That moving drama of the absent bone and the suffering dog is one of the gems of literature for the ministry."

In our preaching we should never permit exports to exceed imports, lest our ministerial economics collapse. With the zest, discrimination, patience, and persistence of connoisseurs in search of curios, we should gather and garner the finest illustrations we can find. In other words, we should cultivate the habit of hoarding.

Before proceeding to explore this branch of our study, let us pause for a while to remind ourselves of several undoubted gains certain to result from this provident practice.

The first gain is obvious. Storing our illustrations helps us to avoid that appalling waste of pictorial matter which unharvested reading inevitably entails. Many ministers, it seems to me, allow an unconscionable amount of illustrative potential to slip through their mental fingers because of failure to collate and classify and store it up. How different was Dr. Sangster! The anonymous author of a brief sketch of his life observes:

His most striking ability in preaching was his power of illustration. This was no happy knack; it was the result of many years of careful preparation. From his student days he had carefully noted all telling stories and put them in a file under subjects. This grew with the years until a huge file, four feet high, could barely contain them. Every incident of human life that had wisdom, or pith, or that showed man at his best or his worst, or, as he usually is, somewhere between

143

THE ART OF ILLUSTRATING SERMONS

the two—each incident was filed away ready for use when the occasion should arise.[1]

In all this I am assuming that we wish to keep our illustrations. There are preachers who, from time to time, destroy their sermon manuscripts, illustrations and all. William Robertson Nicoll did that. Before leaving Kelso for London, to begin his meteoric career as a religious journalist and editor, he made a bonfire of all his pulpit notes. James Denney did the same. At the close of his ministry in Broughty Ferry, he consigned to the flames every discourse he had written. Thomas Champness sinned similarly. Traveling north by train to Newcastle one day and crossing the bridge that spans the Tyne, he opened the carriage window and tossed out a bundle of memoranda representing the ministerial toil of years.

With all deference, one cannot but feel that that is very foolish. Even if born of the healthy fear that in later life we may be tempted to fall back too often on our earlier work and so lose freshness and force, the practice cannot be justified. The tangible results of our ministry are meager enough, God knows, and admittedly a pile of papers, yellowed by the years, is not much of a memento of work accomplished; but it is at least something to hold against oblivion, a pathetic little relic of the unreturning past.

The second gain accruing from the hoarding of illustrations is that it assists one toward a truer appraisal of them. On a first reading or writing of them, we shall very probably overestimate them. Then they may well seem of more worth than they actually are, and when we examine them again after a lapse of time we may modify our opinion of them considerably. Some illustrations, like some kinds of apples, improve with storing; others, like flowers, wilt and wither as the days wear on. By and by we are able to tell the one from the other and to weed them out accordingly. "Crab apple fertility" in the production of il-

[1] *Sangster of Westminster* (London: Marshall, Morgan & Scott, 1961), p. 36.

144

lustrations is not good; we ought to prune the tree and so get better fruit. "When a new illustration seizes on a speaker's imagination," declares David Williamson, "it is tempting to make use of it at the earliest possible moment. The lure should be resisted."

A third gain yielded by the hoarding of pen-pictures is that it gives preaching "background." "Few men," says Emerson, "have any next; they live from hand to mouth, they are without plan, and soon come to the end of their line." It is a mistake to conduct one's preaching on that principle. We ought to have behind us an ample hoard, and then we shall give our hearers the pleasing impression that in the pulpit we speak from opulence and that we have it in our power, if we choose, to be much more pictorially illuminating than we are.

There is a story of an old man who had two sons in the ministry and who, in response to the question as to which of them was the better preacher, is reported to have replied: "Well, George has the better show in the window, but John has the better stock!" Surely the ideal is to have both. For, on the one hand, it is of no use having a good public display if we have nothing on our shelves; and, on the other hand, there is no point whatever in having a lot in the store if we do not exhibit it. In any case, of this we may be certain—we shall never hide from our people the true state of affairs. Sooner or later they are bound to find out. Behind the full window they will detect the empty shelves.

But perhaps the fact is that in this, as in most things, it is possible to err through going to one or other of two extremes. Some preachers store nothing. Their passage through life is strewn with a debris of discarded notes; with the consequence that, as I have said, at the end of the day they have hardly anything to show for all their homiletical labor under the sun. At the opposite pole are those who hoard everything and who are so methodical that they are the slaves of their own complex systems of storage.

145

Occasionally, of course, there is a tendency to swing from the one extreme to the other—a familiar phenomenon in human behavior. Carl S. Patton, for example, has confessed that this happened to him.

For some years after I began to preach, I tried every filing system I heard of. I kept cutting out stuff and filing it away, under the impression that I must be business-like, only to find afterwards that I didn't know where the material was or that I didn't want it. At the end of the first twenty years of my ministry I filed all the sermons I had written up to that time—in the incinerator! [2]

In between these extravagant extremes lies the golden mean, and it is for us to endeavor to discover it.

So much, then, for the gains of hoarding illustrations. Now let us review various methods of storage, inquiring which is the most practical and advantageous, and noting in conclusion how the system here recommended works out.

First look at seven modes of stocking illustrations.

Some store them in memory alone. This was the practice of W. L. Watkinson. Somewhat surprisingly, it was also that of F. W. Boreham, to whom perhaps the modern pulpit is indebted as much as to any other for a wealth of delightful illustrations. I once asked him how he hoarded his pictorial materials, and he replied by tapping his brow with his forefinger and assuring me that his head was his only illustrative hive. His sole collection of illustrations lay in recollection.

Nor, where such men are concerned, is the procedure as hazardous as it might seem. It is nothing short of amazing how receptive, retentive, and ready some memories are. Cynddylan Jones, for instance, a notable Welsh preacher of a former day, claimed to be able to recall clearly the contents of the five and a half tons of books he had read. Surely a phenomenal feat! Not many of us could match it. On the contrary, most of us feel rather like the

---

[2] *The Preparation and Delivery of Sermons* (Chicago: Willett, Clark & Co., 1938), p. 3.

man who referred bitterly to his memory as "that traitor," and are fain to confess that we have a "good forgettory." We are all prone at times to define our memory as the "thing we forget with," and to deplore the loss of the mass of excellent illustrative matter which slips through the sieve of our minds, leaving not a rack behind. Alexander Whyte was wont to complain that he had "the worst memory in Edinburgh," and to acknowledge to his student friends: "No one knows the labour that my memory has cost me."

Unless, therefore, we belong to the favored few on whom a smiling fortune has conferred a photographic faculty for receiving immediate, accurate, and durable impressions, we would be well advised to steer clear altogether of the memory method of storing our stories, or at least to pay heed in this connection to the wise words of C. O. Eldridge: "It is necessary to train the memory till it becomes like a well-arranged store in which every article is in place, ready at call."

Some, again, store illustrations in scrapbooks. This method is recommended with certain reservations by D. C. Bryan. It has the merit of being a great time-saver. Clipping out a pictorial paragraph and pasting it into a homiletic holdall is the task of but a minute or two, and may even be delegated to a helpful friend. Other techniques employed in hoarding word-pictures are sometimes gluttonous of the hours. Not so this one. Busy, as we preachers ought ever to be, fighting all the while a losing battle with the clock, we may well be grateful for a simple, time-saving device for preserving our pictorial stock.

Another thing in favor of the scrapbook method is that illustrations snipped thus from the printed page and stuck between two stiff boards take up so small an amount of room. They have a certain tabloid compactness. They fill but a little space. And, as every seasoned preacher knows, there are occasions when to have them in this light and portable form is a distinct advantage.

Yet a further thing to be said for this system of storage is that it insures that the sermon-paintings shall be stocked in a full and finished fashion. When we commit a story to memory or make but sketchy notes of it, we may inadvertently, when relating it, leave out some vital detail for lack of which, later on, the whole point of the narrative may be missed. When, however, the illustration we wish to store is prefabricated and has just to be cut out and gummed into a scrapbook, we are able to store the whole illustration in a minimum of language, and may thus enter into other men's labors and reap the harvest of their toil.

For all that, this method cannot be commended without grave qualification. There is one fatal objection to it. It calls for the destruction of the books in one's library, a species of vandalism which no lover of good literature can contemplate without horror. In the case of newspapers and magazines, the mutilation may not matter very much. Fugitive literature anyway, it would soon be consigned to the scrapheap if it did not find its way into the scrapbook. But where the volumes on our bookshelves are concerned, it is very different. Such volumes are meant to last for more than a lifetime, and to use the scissors on their fair pages is sheer savagery.

If, therefore, we decide to store our stories like this, we should confine our butchery to the ephemeral effusions of the press. Newspapers and journals may, after we have read them, quite properly be put to the knife, but we ought to have mercy on our precious volumes. When tempted in the interests of the storage of illustrations to subject them to dissection, each of us ought to tell himself firmly and decisively: "Bookman, spare that tome!"

Once more, some store them in commonplace books, books of one's occasional thoughts and favorite quotations. This was Phillips Brooks's method, and it has been that of many another. The value of such homemade volumes is enormous. Spurgeon indeed counseled his students to use commonplace books, contending that if they did not they ran a serious risk of becoming commonplace themselves. To which John Oman adds the counterbalancing advice: "We must have a high standard of recruiting, if a commonplace book in the ancient sense of what is of general value is not to degenerate into a book of commonplaces in the modern sense." Manifestly, too, there must be some sort of classification of the items in the collection if it is to be of prompt and efficient service. As Dr. Sangster forcefully expressed it: "A commonplace book crammed with unclassified matter is no better than a bin!"

Given, then, these two things—a high standard of recruiting and some kind of classification—such a collection can in truth contribute greatly to the attractiveness and effectiveness of our sermons. The labor of transcribing entries, especially if done by longhand, can doubtless become a severe weariness to the flesh. Let us hope that by God's grace it may likewise prove a bracing discipline and development of the mind and spirit; and, in any case, the gains derived from the practice far outweigh the pains incurred. "I have always been grateful," owns Benjamin P. Browne, "for Dr. James Black's suggestion that a sizable ledger may serve to keep enormous materials easily available between two covers."

Some store them in envelopes. This was D. L. Moody's method. Its virtues are that, like the scrapbook system, it is time-sparing and labor-saving, and that it provides the preacher with a handy mode of packing pictorial baggage. But there is much to be urged against it. One strong objection is that envelopes so soon get worn and torn, dog-eared and shabby, through overmuch fingering. Another is that they are so easily mislaid and lost. A third is that, as illustrations multiply and the number of envelopes required to contain them increases proportionately, we tend in time to become in our studies a species of homiletic postman— men of letters in the wrong sense—literally enveloped by envelopes! All things considered, perhaps these drawbacks may be deemed sufficient to put us off the practice altogether.

Some store them in filing cabinets. This method was adopted and advocated by preachers as widely different as A. T. Pierson, Henry Sloane Coffin, and Leslie Weatherhead. In relation to

149

the sermon illustration, "File it, don't defile it," was their slogan. Pierson's biographer writes thus of his mode of sermon storage: "In his study at home were a hundred large boxes, indexed according to important subjects and letters of the alphabet—not a complicated system—but one for ready reference." Those boxes were the crude precursors of the modern filing cabinet. Dr. Coffin and Dr. Weatherhead were of a later generation, and their modes of stocking illustrations were more sophisticated and up-to-date, but they were based on the same principle. "I am constantly on the lookout for illustrations," confessed Dr. Coffin, "and have for years entered on library-cards quotations from my reading. It is no use trusting one's memory, and if laziness rebels at the task of storing up illustrative material against a future need, I quote to myself a verse from Proverbs: 'The slothful man roasteth not that which he took in hunting.' " Dr. Weatherhead also employs that method. He boasts of his infallible filing system "by which I can have on my desk in ten minutes anything I have ever read on any relevant subject on religion."

Attempted on an ambitious scale, this mode calls for cumbersome, auxiliary machinery—an elaborate card index system and an intricate arrangement of cross-references. Actually, I suppose, when it becomes as complex and comprehensive as that, one would need a private secretary to keep up with it! Yet, most certainly, if we can manage things ourselves, it is a very workmanlike way in which to handle a large mass of pictorial matter.

Nevertheless, several damaging criticisms can be leveled at it. For one thing, illustrations hoarded in this manner are not conveniently portable. A man cannot carry a filing cabinet about with him, and to extract some of its contents on occasion for use as sermon notes is to run the risk of mislaying them or of failing to return them to their proper places. For another thing, by utilizing some such highly intricate mechanical system—"that snug arrangement of labeled and classified data, so dear to the routine mind"—we tend ourselves to become mechanical. May I go further and, copying Esaias, be "very bold" and say that in

150

my judgment the Lord does not often visit with lubricating unction the soul of the preacher who is overmethodical, too self-consciously systematic—for the simple reason that such a person is almost certain to be so preoccupied with the mere mechanics of the ministry as more or less to shut himself off from the divine afflatus?

There are men among us who would reduce everything to a system. Properly impressed with the value and importance of order, they make a fetish of it. Nothing that is not tabbed and ticketed, dated and docketed, filed and foldered is to be found in their studies outside the waste basket. Well, there is a legitimate place in sermon preparation for system, method, classification, tabulation, organization, and the like; but it must always be a subordinate place. The harness must never be suffered to become too heavy for the horse, and things must not be so classified and systematized that there is no spirit left in them. The rule is that we should be methodical, but that we should not permit ourselves to become the victims of our own passion for order. Taking Samuel Smiles's excellent advice, we should have "a place for everything and everything in its place." We should master our materials and not let them master us.

But if, after all, we find that our minds do not readily "gear themselves into" such elaborate and ingenious modes of storing word-pictures, we need not be unduly bothered about it. We are in good company. "Don't be hectored," writes James Black "into believing that you ought to adopt those artificial docketing methods that suit a businessman or a railway ticket-office—schedules, systems, fancy drawers with tickets on wires. . . . Personally, that type of thing would wring me as dry as a sucked orange!" A practice threatening to reduce the preacher to so dehydrated a condition can hardly be heartily approved of!

Some store them in libraries. This was one of the methods employed by W. E. Sangster, and there is certainly much to be said for it. It does not demand the literary dissection called for by other modes of storage, and it enables us as preachers to have

151

within convenient reach a wide range of illustrative materials. All we have to do is underline or otherwise mark the pictorial passages we prize in books we read—which, of course, are our own property. Then, on the blank pages at the back of each, or on the inside covers, set down a short note of the subject and the number of the page on which the illustrative item appears. Fuller particulars—the name of the author, the title and number of the volume, and so on—can be ledgered later in a general index in which the entire pictorial content of a library is alphabetically tabulated under proper headings, every word-picture being, as Sangster himself phrased it, "on call" at a moment's notice. Urgently in need of some specific illustration, all we have to do, as we sit in our book-lined study, is to consult the general index, stretch for the volume required, turn to the page indicated, and there it is.

Yet the method has one defect. The library has to be there. For the man in a settled pastorate, building his sermons week by week within the same four walls, this system may be all right. But who of us can be absolutely certain that, faced with an immediately impending ministerial appointment, he will always have his library at arm's length? And what of those who habitually exercise an itinerant ministry and are scarcely ever at home? Lacking the transport facilities of the snail, a man cannot carry his library about with him on his back; and, as for a general index, of what use would that be to anyone if the books listed in it were a thousand miles away? On the other side of the world from where we normally reside, and where therefore the large majority of our books may be presumed to be located, we may find ourselves in urgent need of some particular word-picture which we can vaguely recall but cannot distinctly recollect; and, oh, how tantalizing a half-remembered illustration can be!

There, then, are the six conventional methods of storing pictorial preaching materials. There is something to be said for storing them in memory, in scrapbooks, in commonplace books, in envelopes or folders, in filing cabinets, and in libraries; but each of these methods has its own peculiar drawbacks and disadvantages.

Is there some other method of storing them less open to criticism and more satisfactory in operation? There is—provided one is prepared for long-range planning in the ministry.

Here is the method. The first thing to be done is to furnish ourselves with large Bibles, with wide margins or interleaving, and these we must, of course, study carefully, prayerfully, systematically, with such scholarly aids as are available, underlining all the preachable texts or passages. Whenever any such portion strikes us or suggests some possible line of treatment, we should note it at once in the margin or on the spare leaf of the Bible. By this means we shall bit by bit build up a collection of sermon plans. And every now and then we should go through the Bible methodically, combing page after page for new underscorings or marginal comments and from them constructing fresh outlines and likewise collecting and garnering such sermon schemes as appear, on second thoughts, deserving of development and permanence. After that, we should transfer these outlines, arranged in textual order, to large loose-leaf notebooks with stiff covers, typing at the top right-hand corner of each sheet a note to indicate the nature of its contents. To every prospective sermon we should allocate a number of pages equivalent to the number of points we propose to make—two, three, four, five, or six—as the case may be—plus two further pages, to be reserved respectively for the introduction and the conclusion, and labeled accordingly.

To begin with, after being inserted in our loose-leaf books, the pages will look disconcertingly blank, but we must not let that daunt us. Keeping our minds on our specific pictorial requirements as indicated by the gaps in our plans, we shall find before long relevant illustrations leaping out upon us from all sorts of unexpected places and positively clamoring for inclusion in some ripening discourse. If not, word-pictures may be stored for years, perhaps because we do not feel led to preach along the lines they illustrate, or because we judge that we have not as yet completed our quota of sermon substance on the subjects in question. At last, however, their time will come, and we shall fit them into the finished discourses in a fashion of which we shall have something to say later.

Now let us see how all this works out. Take, by way of illustration, three selected samples.

Suppose that, in reading our New Testament, we are impressed by the fact that in it the Aramaic word "Abba," "Father," is transliterated three times (Mark 14:36; Rom. 8:15; Gal. 4:6), and suppose that somehow we sense that we are here on the trail of a sermon. We make a note of the matter in the margin of our Bibles with a view to transferring the entry later to our loose-leaf planbooks. Then our subconscious minds get busy with the theme, and presently pertinent pictorial materials offer themselves for use. We are reading, it may be, a volume of biography, and suddenly we run up against something that strikes us as exactly adaptable to the new plan. It is Paul Sangster's captivating biography of his father and, while turning its pages, we light on this poignant passage which presents a moving picture of the paternal heart. The son writes:

He stood at the end of a bed in a darkened hospital ward where I lay dangerously ill, waiting for an emergency operation which might, or might not, save my life. I was barely conscious, but I could just make out his whispered words: "I can't help you. Why can't I help you? Son, I'd go to hell for you if it would help!" [3]

That, too, we decide, must be included in the relevant section of our outline and it is promptly put there. But our quest for illustrative materials is not yet over. There are gaps in the plan that still need filling. Soon our musing minds, ruminating on the Pauline phrase "the Spirit of adoption" (Rom. 8:15), reflect

[3] Dr. Sangster (London: Epworth Press, 1962), p. 335.

that, unlike the divine Father, human fathers do not always succeed in transmitting their spirits to their sons, and soon we recollect three notable paradigms to illuminate the point. Presently our pictorial paragraph shapes itself something like this:

Not always can human fathers contrive to communicate their spirits to their sons. In biography illustrations of this abound. Richard Cromwell was not of the same spirit as his father Oliver. Robert Wiedemann Barrett Browning, for all his high-sounding name, was not of the same spirit as his sire the poet. Thomas Spurgeon, though no mean preacher, was not of the same spirit as his illustrious parent Charles Haddon Spurgeon. No. Human fathers do not always manage to convey their spirits to their sons. But God can and does! We "have received the Spirit of adoption, whereby we cry, Abba, Father" (Rom. 8:15).

Furnished with such luminous illustrations, the outline is almost ready for the final brushwork which will make it a finished product.

Or suppose that, browsing in the Bible, our roving eyes light on that magnificent passage in which, as the old Puritan pithily put it, "Paul, penniless, hands over the title-deeds of the universe"—"All things are yours; whether Paul, or Apollos, or Cephas, or the world, or life, or death, or things present, or things to come; all are yours; and ye are Christ's; and Christ is God's" (I Cor. 3:21-23). Immediately we are gripped by the conviction that we are meant to preach on that passage, and a possible title for the sermon suggests itself—"Reading the Will." Picturing the apostle telling his readers that they have become God's heritors through the death of Christ, we revolve the subject in our thoughts until at last we reach the conclusion that the text falls very naturally, like Gaul, into three parts. Paul tells his converts that: (1) all the ministries of the Christian Church are theirs ("Paul, Apollos, Cephas"); (2) all the experiences of human existence are theirs ("the world, life, death"); and (3) all the realities of time and eternity are theirs ("things present, things to come"). Soon the outline finds its way into our plan-books, and we begin to keep a sharp lookout for pertinent illustrative matter.

We have not long to wait. Shortly afterward we go, it may be, into Wolverhampton Art Gallery, and there we see a picture which casts a spell upon us. It is called "The Flaw in the Will," and it depicts a young widow, garbed in black, a baby in her arms. She is consulting an old lawyer in his office. Together they are scanning a legal document with manifest concern. There seems to be some grave and grievous error. The young widow's title to the estate of her late husband is in dispute. In the will there is a fatal flaw. Instinctively we feel that, antithetically applied, that painting may act as a word-picture for our new sermon. Thank God, there is no flaw in *his* will!

Later on, perhaps, we visit one of the stately homes of England and, while so doing, pick up some fascinating information and make certain illuminating observations which together help to build up an illustration in our minds. At once we jot down notes in our sketch-book, and afterward paint the full word-picture as well as we can, eventually transcribing it to our loose-leaf books in some such form as this:

Imagine a lordly castle standing in the midst of a great estate. Around it lie gardens and fields, woods and hills, and through its grounds runs a river. And now imagine that the duke, the titular owner of the place, sits in one of the splendid apartments of the castle. But he is blind, we will suppose, and cannot see the beauty of the scenes around him; deaf, and cannot hear the laughter of the rippling water or the music of the birds; rheumatic, chained to his chair by pain and utterly unable to move freely about his ample acres. Imagine, further, that among the tenantry on the estate lives a little lad of nine or ten, whose delight it is to wander through the fields, ramble in the woods, and wade and swim in the river. Now, tell me, which of these two really owns the castle? It is not the duke. Oh, no! It is the little fellow who is able to enjoy it to the full!

This likewise, we consider, merits a corner in our sermon outline and is duly posted there.

Still in search of relevant pictorial substance related to our sermon, "Reading the Will," we chance to take up a volume of sermons entitled Things New and Old, by J. R. S. Wilson; and, as we finger its pages, we hit upon this fascinating paragraph. The preacher is in Edinburgh, and he cries:

Yonder on the Pentland Hills is where the Covenanting fathers met to worship according to their conscience. Those were great days and many stories are told of them. One fine morning a barefoot lass was making her way up over a heather track, when she was encountered by a trooper officer. He stopped her and said: "Whither away, my lass, so early in the morning and in such haste?" "Oh, sir," she said, "I have heard of the death of my Elder Brother, and I go to hear what He has left me in His will." "A thrifty queyne," he said. And so pleased was he that he gave her a silver piece of money. But he little knew what she meant. She was making her way to a conventicle in some fold of the heather hills. Soon she would take into her trembling hands the symbol of the shed blood of that Elder Brother and she would listen as the preacher expounded to them, seated on the hillside, the rich treasures of the covenant of God sealed in the precious blood of His dear Son.[4]

Space, we resolve, will simply have to be found for that; and so, piece by piece, the blanks in the plan are filled in, and the sermon grows apace.

Or—to offer a final instance of how the system works out—it may be that at Christmastime some year, when composing a sermon on the Advent theme, we select as text Matt. 1:21: "Thou shalt call his name Jesus: for he shall save his people from their sins." Titling the discourse, "The Christening of Christ," we mean in it to press the point that each of us must name Christ for himself, giving him an appellation signifying

[4] J. R. S. Wilson, Things New and Old (London: Pickering & Inglis, 1943), p. 64.

what he means to us and has done for us in our personal lives. To call him, as some do, "hero," "genius," "religious leader," and so on, while true, is not enough. We must find other names for him or fail altogether to take the full measure of his greatness. What, then, we may ask, shall we call him, and why? And the answer we shall offer is fourfold. We shall call him: (1) Savior, because he salves our guilty consciences; (2) Master, because he controls our wayward wills; (3) Teacher, because he instructs our ignorant minds; (4) Lover, because he captivates our fickle hearts.

That is, we feel, a workman-like plan deserving of a niche in our loose-leaf books. In it goes, and once again our busy brains strum on that string of thought. Some names, we conclude upon reflection, have little or no relation to the personalities or activities of their possessors. God's names, however, not only designate but describe. Brooding over the matter, we remember noticing a number of names which had a purely fortuitous, perhaps even whimsical, consonance with the characters or occupations of those who bore them. And gradually the following topical illustration forms itself in our minds:

It is a fact which I dare say many of you have noticed that some people's names seem to accord most amusingly with the nature of their trades or professions. A few sparkling examples have recently come within range of my own observation. Outside a house in a Lancashire town, for instance, I saw a brass plate with this inscription: "F. Sharp: Piano-tuner." Above a shop in a city in the Midlands I read: "A. Codd: Fishmonger." Near where I live there is a postmaster named Mr. Stamps!

To be sure, such odd correspondences between a man's calling and what he happens to be called are mere coincidences. But it is not always so. A person may be named "Mason" because one of his forefathers wielded a chisel, or "Miller" because among his ancestors was someone whose business it was to grind flour, or "Butler" because a remote progenitor may have acted in that capacity.

In the Bible, however, names mean much more than that. They have a moral and spiritual significance. And among all the names in the sacred literature infinitely the noblest is the name "Jesus."

It may very well be that that is the only pictorial item on that topic we happen to have at the time. So we enter the word-picture in our loose-leaf books and leave it there for awhile. Ere long, however, we hear a story that strikes us as being designed for that outline as the glove is designed for the hand.

In Sydney, Australia, a preacher once met an old lady who told him a touching tale. It was about a lad who went from that city to London many years ago to seek his fortune. He had not been there long when he was smitten with disease. Taken to a hospital, he was found to be beyond human skill. As the end drew near, the sufferer began to behave in a manner which mystified the hospital staff. Always he kept crying: "Fresh water! Fresh water! Fresh water!" They brought him water, cool and sparkling from the tap, but he pushed it aside and still kept calling out: "Fresh water! Fresh water! Fresh water!" Completely nonplussed, the staff did everything in their power to persuade him that the water they were offering him was absolutely fresh. Yet always he refused it with what feeble strength he had, and went on exclaiming: "Fresh water! Fresh water! Fresh water!" At last the doctors and nurses got in touch with a friend of the young man, who had known him as a boy in Australia, asking if he could help to solve the mystery. "Fresh water!" his friend mused. "So he goes on calling for fresh water! Well, there was a *Miss* Freshwater who used to be his Sunday-school teacher when he was a lad in Sydney. I wonder if it is for her he is calling?" They thought it possible. So without delay they cabled to the lady in question, explaining the situation, and begging for an immediate reply. At once she wired back: "Freshwater still loves you and is praying for you." The message was read to the young man and, as he listened to it, a faint smile played upon his lips. He stopped calling out as before; and, after a little, slipped quietly away, upheld by the love and prayers of his former Sunday-school teacher. There was much in that name. It stood for something in the youth's mind.

159

It reminded him of Jesus. And, incidentally, the old lady who told the preacher the story was Miss Freshwater herself!

There, once more, is thrillingly relevant illustrative material for our sermon planbook.

Not even yet, however, is our hunt for apposite pictorial substance at an end. We have still to find an illustration for point number four, and in one of the works of John Drinkwater we lay our finger on the very thing we want. Discussing Mary, Queen of Scots, and referring to her erotic instability and matrimonial infidelities, Drinkwater makes this discerning and understanding comment: "She never had a lover great enough to establish her heart." Jesus *is* great enough to do that! He *can* stabilize our emotions, captivate our affections, and strengthen our wavering wills to the exclusion of every lesser love.

Before turning from this topic of storing illustrations, there is one further point to be taken up. What is to happen to those whether derived from literature, drawn from life, or devised by the imagination, for which, when first found or framed, no absolutely appropriate place exists in any of the plans in our collection? Are we to try to force such illustrative items into outlines which they do not quite fit, or are we to fling them away because we do not happen to have an immediate vacancy for them? Neither of these courses is to be commended. Rather must we provide some temporary anchorage for such "floating" illustrations until we can find for them a homiletic haven. A separate stout-backed loose-leaf book will do. Posted in alphabetical order of subjects within such covers, stray illustrations of that sort can be kept safe until precisely the right setting for them is available.

Assuming, then, that we are in urgent need of some specific sermon and that we feel divinely directed to one in particular, for which we have ample illustrative materials, the next task is to fit them in to the finished discourse. If we have taken proper pains with the gradual amassing of the materials in our planbook, admitting nothing which is not strictly relevant, we ought to have on hand exactly what we need. Of one master of the preacher's craft it was said that "he chose his illustrations as a surgeon selects the instruments necessary for an operation." A surgeon does not scratch about looking for the right instruments when the patient is on the table. He sees to it that they are ready beforehand. So should we in this matter of sermon illustrations; and if, as I say, we have carefully sifted the pictorial materials prior to placing them in our planbook, they will be there when wanted.

161

6

Fitting Them In

How many illustrations should a sermon have? That is a point
on which it would patently be unwise to pontificate. On it experts differ and where they disagree dogmatism is usually dangerous. In any case, regimentation in this direction would tend
to produce a mechanical and stereotyped ministry, with sermons
as uniform and standardized as Ford cars. W. E. Sangster ex-
pressly warns us against the unwisdom of always having the same
number of illustrations in our addresses. That caution deserves
respectful consideration. Yet there are certain governing principles which can confidently be laid down as a guide to one's
general practice along this line.

Some men preach conservatory sermons—all windows. They
illustrate, it would seem, merely for the sake of illustrating.
Listening to their sermons is like watching a swift-running film
in which scene follows scene in rapid succession. This is to
overdo a good thing. In his recently published and racily written
autobiography, Four Score and More, A. Lindsay Glegg observes: "Illustrations have been likened to windows that let in
the light, but that is no reason why our addresses should be like
the old Crystal Palace!"

On the other hand, there are ministers whose sermons are
as windowless as prisons. Clarence E. Macartney compares their
discourses to something of that sort. "In Russian Caucasia," he
says, "one can see strange-looking houses. They are built like a

tower, solid, substantial, lofty, but without a window." That, again, is too sweeping a swing of the pendulum.

Somewhere in between the two extremes lies the happy medium. Tyrrell Green, in his day, maintained that "no sermon to an adult congregation should contain more than one illustration." That is a ruling to which few modern preachers, with any pictorial sensibility, would subscribe. A better plan is that proposed by W. L. Watkinson. He recommends that as a rule one illustration should be used to drive home each point of the sermon. A. Lindsay Glegg—to quote him again—suggests that it is a good thing to put three illustrations into every discourse, and in the case of the classical "three decker" type of outline that is how Watkinson's proposal would work out. In line with this is the pronouncement on the matter by an old Scottish sermon-taster of my acquaintance who insists that every discourse should be equipped, as he puts it, with "three pints and three pickters!"

In any case, whatever we decide about a convenient number for insertion, we should not suffer ourselves to become the victims of our own systems, tying our hands with our own red tape. "I know a minister," says Sangster, "who uses illustrations regularly and puts the same number into each of his sermons; and, from his methods, I am bound to conclude that he does this designedly. He appears to illustrate simply because it is considered proper to illustrate. He seems to be quite satisfied provided he puts in the requisite number."

Never ought we to permit ourselves to be as hidebound by habit as that. Always we should employ illustrations, not just for the sake of doing so, but because we have some vital purpose in view; and we should leave the question as to the exact number of word-paintings to be included in any given sermon to be dictated by the exigencies of the case. By all means, let us put pictures into our discourses, but there is no need to turn every one of them into a kind of Sunday picture section. So much for the number of illustrations.

And if anyone asks precisely where in the sermon it is proper to illustrate, the answer is: "Wherever illustration is necessary—at the beginning, in the development, or at the close." An effective illustration is never out of place. It can provide an arresting opening for the discourse, gripping the hearers' attention from the start, and leading straight to a discussion of the theme. It can help, as we have seen in the first chapter, to elucidate obscure points, to add interest and liveliness to our treatment of the subject, and to embellish the sermon with a touch of beauty which will enhance its popular appeal. It can also bring things to a brisk issue, compel the listeners to face up to a challenge from which they would fain escape and constrain them toward commitment to Christ. Anything that can do this is never out of place in a sermon.

Perhaps it may be as well at this point to issue certain cautions concerning the misuse of illustrations.

The first is that of employing word-pictures *which are worn out and outworn.* Antiquated anecdotes and stale stories of all kinds should be respectfully laid to rest. Having served their day and generation, it is high time they fell asleep. Doubtless, to be sure, when first recounted, such narratives were arresting and attractive enough, otherwise there would hardly have been such a "run" on them. But now, through overmuch recounting, they have become effete and threadbare, and have quite lost the freshness and force of unfamiliarity.

We ought, of course, to recognize that what is trite and commonplace and outmoded to one person may seem original and novel and gripping to another; nevertheless it is not wise to inflict upon a longsuffering congregation an illustration which we have good reason to believe is too well known to be really interesting to the majority of our hearers, just because we suspect, perhaps rightly, that some of the younger folk are unfamiliar with it. "Novelty," remarked C. Wood, "always attracts, overfamiliarity always repels." That is a saying well worth pondering in relation to the telling of these stock stories. They should be pensioned off. John Watson once declared, doubtless with his tongue in his cheek, that Protestantism too could do with an official index expurgatorius whose central authority would decree at times that "such and such anecdotes, having been worn threadbare, are now withdrawn from circulation."

Very likely, as I have just suggested, such anecdotes were most effective when first used; but, with the lapse of time, each of them has become, like Scott's *Marmion*, "an old tale, and often told." And whenever, unmindful of its longevity and over-familiarity, we are foolish enough to embark in the pulpit upon the telling of such a tale, the congregation tends to grow restive and weary, sharing no doubt in this regard the feelings of T. Harwood Pattison: "Who has not wished that Michelangelo had left the angel to slumber in the stone and said not a word about it?"

Nothing could be to us as preachers more devastatingly disconcerting than to depend on some particular illustration to sustain popular interest in a discourse only to discover in the actual delivery of it, that we have been forestalled; that in truth through frequent repetition in sermons the story has become so well known to our hearers as almost to have degenerated into a jest. An amusing case of this is instanced by Arthur Porritt in his volume of reminiscences, *The Best I Remember*. It is as follows:

Some time ago, when the church I attend was without a minister for about a year, we had a procession of preachers through the pulpit. One after another told, as a children's address, a story about a boy who presented his mother with a bill for 2/6d, setting out the charges for running errands, chopping wood, cleaning knives and other odd chores. The mother paid the 2/6d, but along with the cash presented her bill—"For caring for Fred for nine years, feeding him, clothing him, nursing him, taking him on holidays, etc., £0:0:0." It was quite a nice little moral story, and on first hearing was very effective. But as one "supply" preacher after another told the story its lustre dimmed and at last we found it interesting to watch for variations in the boy's bill. Eventually, when a good friend of my own, the Reverend J. G., supplied the pulpit and began his children's address with the threadbare story, there were smiles all over the church. Next day, I met J. G. in a restaurant, and congratulated him on his children's address. He seemed pleased. Then I added: "Well, I'll put it this way—of all the ten men who have told that story from our pulpit in the last twelve months, you told it the best." [1]

To avoid similar discomfiture we would do well to check up, where we can, on the possible familiarity to our hearers of any illustrations we intend to introduce into a forthcoming sermon. Of William Quayle it was said that "his illustrations were as fresh as some flower he had plucked on the way to the pulpit." This should be our objective.

Another mistake to avoid is that of *retailing in the pulpit improbable anecdotes* which, in the words of the colloquialism, "take some believing." "Often," remarks David Williamson, "one has heard stories related by speakers which are so exaggerated or carelessly narrated that they put a strain upon one's credulity." Never ought we in our preaching to tell for truth tales the credibility of which is likely to be suspected by every thinking person in our audience, remembering that even the most ordinary men and women have an uncanny knack of knowing when a story is false, notwithstanding the wily efforts of the narrator to persuade them to the contrary. One would think they had a sort of lie detector inside them, by which they sense, almost infallibly, though they could not tell how, that what purports to be fact is pure fiction. Oftentimes they are quicker in realizing this than we preachers ourselves, for we are apt to be blinded by our bias in favor of a good story, irrespective of its truth or falsity, and to give it the benefit of any doubt there may be about it because of its possible homiletic serviceableness. However that may be, we must always respect our people's mental

[1] (London: Cassell & Co., 1922), pp. 234-35.

powers and never treat the members of our congregations as if they did not possess the critical intelligence of the kindergarten. We recall John Gay's cautionary couplet:

Lest men suspect your tale untrue,
Keep probability in view.

Now and then, indeed, we may find it hard to decide offhand whether a story reported to us as true actually is so. Notoriously, truth is stranger than fiction, and he is a bold man who lightly concludes that a thing is impossible simply because he thinks it could not happen.

Consider a case in point.

A ministerial colleague of mine once served as chaplain in a great prison. Among the convicts to whom he had access in the performance of his duties was a man, convicted on a grave charge, who, on close acquaintance following numerous interviews, turned out to be a very different sort of person from the general run of the prisoners. Having won his confidence, my friend put to him point-blank the question: "Did you, or did you not, commit the crime for which you were sentenced?" The stock answer among convicts to such an inquiry is, of course, "No," and not much faith is usually placed in it; but somehow when this man said it, the negative sounded convincing. The chaplain offered to take the matter up, but the convict dissuaded him, explaining that he had been so long in captivity that liberty had lost its charm for him and that, in any case, if discharged, he would have nowhere to go. Nevertheless, the prisoner continued to protest his innocence. Then a day came when he suddenly sickened and died. In accordance with prison procedure, he was buried in a plain board coffin within the grounds of the jail. Only the four warders who carried the body and my friend were present at the funeral. It was a glorious summer day, and as the casket was being borne on the shoulders of the warders to its last resting-place, a white dove suddenly flew over the high wall, circled overhead for a while, and eventually settled on the coffin lid, remaining there until the bearers halted at the graveside. After that it took to the air again and wheeled round and round until the simple ceremony was over. When telling me the story, my friend's comment was choice: "God had *his* mourner at the funeral!"

Now there is no denying that that narrative does seem fantastically improbable. Although I first heard it many years ago, I confess that still to myself it appears a trumped-up tale. Yet I have it on the authority of one whose utter truthfulness it would be impossible for me to impugn; one, moreover, who was in an excellent position to know the facts. So we need to be watchful in drawing our conclusions as to the factuality or falsity of the stories we purpose to use.

Incidents of the type I have just cited are, however, extremely exceptional. As a rule common sense is an almost infallible guide in such matters; and if, having weighed the evidence on both sides and made up our minds that the likelihood is that some particular story is apocryphal, we still feel that it possesses distinct value as pictorial material for a discourse and decide to include it, the best thing to do is to be quite frank about it, stating candidly as we start to tell it that we do not accept the tale as factual, but that for the purpose of our exposition of the truth under review we intend to utilize it all the same. Here is an example of such handling of a highly dubious story:

There is an altogether improbable but very suggestive story of how a business gentleman, living in an English provincial town, came down to breakfast one morning to make a most disconcerting discovery. Picking up the newspaper, he glanced through its contents casually enough, until all at once his eye lighted on something that shocked him out of his complacency and sent a shiver down his spine! There, among the obituary notices, stood his own name! By some incredible mischance his death had been reported in the press. With thumping heart, he read the little paragraph through once or twice, as though incapable of crediting the testimony of his own senses. Then, as the truth dawned upon him, he sprang from his chair, stormed across the room, lifted the telephone receiver and asked to be put through at once to the editor's office. In due course the newspaperman made known his presence at the other end of the line. "My name is Brown," blazed the businessman, "John Brown!" "Good morning, Mr. Brown," responded the editor, "what can we do for you?" "Do for me?" snapped Brown. "It's not what you can do for me, it's what you've done to me." "I don't understand," said the editor, "pray explain." "You've printed the notice of my death in this morning's issue of your paper!" "What!" gasped the editor, "but that's impossible." "It isn't," barked Brown, "you've done it. Look at page three, column five." The editor did. And there, sure enough, among the deaths was the man's name. What was the editor to do? For a moment or two, he hadn't an earthly idea. But then a bright thought came to him. Going back to the phone, he said: "Yes, Mr. Brown, I'm afraid you're right. We have announced your passing in today's issue of our paper, and I'm terribly sorry. But," he added hopefully, "I'll tell you what we'll do—we'll put you in the births column tomorrow!"

Now that is exactly what Jesus does to sinners. He says that they are dead in relation to God, but that they can by his Spirit be born again. He puts them into the spiritual "births column."

That such an alleged occurrence ever really took place is dead against all the probabilities. In fact, I would go further and say most definitely that it did not take place and never could have taken place. Nevertheless, the narrative has real value as a word-picture illustrating the subject of regeneration. Before employing it, however, we ought to be careful not to give the impression that we actually believe it, or people will lose faith in our judgment. We must tell them candidly at the outset that we do not believe it at all, but that we still consider it of genuine worth and too good to be left out. Then our hearers will listen attentively if for no other reason than to see whether their verdict on the credibility and value of the anecdote corresponds with ours.

Incidentally, and as a matter of interest, it is a curious comment on the utter unpredictability of things that after I had written the above categorical denial that such a situation could arise, a news item appeared in the Daily Express of March 1, 1963, which proved that it could. Here is the press clipping:

When twenty-eight-year-old Tony Tysoe picked up his newspaper he read his death notice. It said: "On February 20, suddenly at his home at Heysham-drive, South Oxhey, Anthony R. Tysoe, aged 30. Cremation private." Then three days of chaos began for Tony and his mother. Wreaths arrived at their Hertfordshire home from friends and relatives. Letters of sympathy poured in by every post. Friends arrived on the Tysoe doorstep in full mourning and were shocked when Tony opened the door. Tony said yesterday: "I know —almost certainly—who is responsible. It's a woman, and I think it's a pure case of love and jealousy gone wrong."

Closely akin to the foregoing is the careless practice of not taking the trouble to get one's facts right.

A small inaccuracy can sometimes ruin the effect of an otherwise excellent word-picture. Not long ago a case of this kind came under my own immediate notice. In a sermon class, in which there were several Continental students, I had ventured to refer to what I pronounced an almost perfect illustration with which to begin a sermon on the Resurrection; but, after having read the word-picture aloud, I was surprised, puzzled, and somewhat mortified to sense that some of the students—those from abroad—did not share my enthusiasm for it and that they were, on the contrary, exchanging meaningful glances with one another and evidently enjoying the fact that they had "caught me out." I could not refrain from inquiring as to the cause of this untimely and unseemly mirth. They explained that it arose from the fact that my "perfect" illustration was marred by a mistake. The preacher had stated that a certain town to which he referred was in Switzerland whereas it is really in Italy! I thought it a very minor matter of which to complain, and said so; and yet the fact remained that for these students it utterly spoiled the impression of a superlatively fine word-painting.

Yet another blunder we ought sedulously to avoid is that of using illustrations *not quite in keeping with the dignity of the pulpit.* Whenever we are a bit dubious about the advisability of inserting in a sermon some particularly impressive illustration because we are afraid that by so doing we may offend the sensibilities of our listeners by a breach of propriety, we had better rule it out ruthlessly. As Bishop Taylor Smith said: "Where there's doubt, there's no doubt." It is always a grave error in preaching to sin against good taste. Well worth pondering in this connection are the words of George A. Buttrick: "A sermon without illustrations is like a house without windows. A sermon with trivial or bathetic illustrations is like a house with the windows broken, and the holes stuffed with rags and straw. Let the illustrations always be dignified and worthy of the theme."

Nor must we forget to take warning of another slip we are likely to make—that of *turning too frequently to the same source* for our illustrations. Just as the great painters often specialized in one branch of their art—historical scenes, landscapes, portraiture, still life, and the like—so even the master preachers have tended at times to favor one type of illustration overmuch. Guthrie, if we may judge from his published works, had a peculiar fondness for shipwrecks; Talmage was great on conflagrations and dramatic escapes; Watkinson, unrivaled craftsman though he was in the construction of sermon-paintings based on science, probably overdid it; of Hugh Macmillan one of his regular hearers, exasperated by his excessive use of analogies having to do with insects, is reported to have exclaimed: "I canna bide his spiders!" Upon which the witty Spurgeon comments: "It would be better to give the people a spider or two occasionally, and then to vary the instruction by stories and anecdotes, and similes and metaphors drawn from geology, astronomy, botany, or any of the other sciences which will help to shed a sidelight on Scripture." Let us ever bear in mind that however excellent illustrations may be in themselves, if always extracted from the same source and delivered to the same congregation, they are bound before long to become boring and monotonous. We should be wise, therefore, to vary not only the types of illustrations we employ in our preaching as a whole, but also those that we use in each individual sermon, painting widely different scenes, objects, and persons, applying various colors, altering the shape and size of our canvases, and so on. Thus we shall safeguard ourselves against the peril of the pet picture.

Past still another pitfall we must pick our wary way—that of *illustrating the obvious*. There are fussy preachers who go to a vast amount of trouble to illuminate some patent point on which no one in his senses has ever stood in need of the slightest enlightenment. Of one preacher Denney devastatingly said that "he had a perfectly marvellous gift for the clamorous presentation of the obvious." Others, it would appear, possess a similar talent for the illustration of the obvious. Quite definitely, it is a talent to be buried in a napkin.

Against yet another mistake we must take defensive measures —that of *using illustrations as substitutes for reasoning* rather rather than as supplements to it. To try to prove a point by telling a tale is always perilous. Illustration is not argument; and yet, as we saw in the first chapter, an illustration will go a long way toward substantiating an argument. For, after all, a proposition which can be supported by valid analogy is, by and large, likelier to be true than one which does not admit of such illustrative corroboration. The fact that the image of a man's face appears when he presents himself before a mirror is not in itself compelling evidence that he is alive—if there was only the image to go by it might be taken for an optical illusion or a psychical phenomenon—but, convinced on other grounds that he is alive, we find in the image strong confirmation of the fact. Word-pictures are indeed helpful supplements to thought, but they are no appropriate or adequate substitute for it. In Thomas Fuller's words: "Reasons are the pillars of the fabric of a sermon, but similitudes are the windows which give the best lights." A window is not a wall. If it lets in light, it serves its purpose and fulfills its function, and no more may legitimately be expected of it. We should never attempt to compel a window to hold up a roof. To force it to bear a weight it was not designed to carry is but to crack and crush it and to cause the total structure to collapse. Sermon-paintings are meant to be the windows of our discourses; we must not expect from a window the supporting power of a wall.

Making the sermon match the illustration, rather than the illustration the sermon, is a further fault to be eschewed. Earlier in these pages we noted that there are occasions when it is permissible and even desirable to use a story or incident as a starting point for a whole address. But the practice is fraught with peril and can only be adopted with the greatest caution. Always it must be the rare exception rather than the rule. "There are some preachers," says George Johnstone Jeffrey, "whose method of sermon preparation seems to be the search for three anecdotes, setting them down like three islands in a homiletical sea, the rest of the sermon consisting in swimming breathlessly from one to the other, in the lively hope of coming safe to land." Provided the discourse as a whole is firmly planted on the Bible, the fact that it owes its origin to an illustration or to a series of illustrations does not, as we have observed, very much matter. The danger is, however, that if we start too often from a story, we may end by referring to the Scriptures simply in an effort to bolster up some fancy theory of our own. This makes the text, in John A. Hutton's phrase, a mere pretext for something we want to say instead of what it should be—the creative idea and motivating principle of our discourse. A good working plan is always to give priority to the Word of God. Beginning with that, we should employ pictorial materials only to illuminate and reinforce a truth which it teaches or a duty which it enjoins. Subordinating the sermon to the illustration may be compared to a man calling at the tailor's for a ready-made suit (the sort of suit which, as the wit said, fits everybody—and nobody); but then, finding that the only suit which takes his eye is far too

173

THE ART OF ILLUSTRATING SERMONS

big for him, says to the assistant: "Set it aside for me. At the moment it is too large. I will go home and eat like a wolf for a while and when I come back it will fit me." What would the reply be? Would it not be something like this? "No, sir, if you really do want the suit, it will be much simpler for us to cut it down to your precise measurements than for you to try to accommodate your figure to its present size." Just so in preaching. We should not, as a rule, seek to make the sermon match the illustration, but rather the illustration the sermon.

There is another obstacle of which we must beware—that of using an *illustration which draws attention to itself* at the expense of the message. This is a tempting trap, for the very fineness, fitness, and forcefulness of the anecdote may induce us, against our better judgment, to accord it too much space and place in the sermon to the detriment of the discourse as a whole. To do so is rash and ruinous. We should never forget that a diverting story may turn out to be diverting in more ways than one. Unless the word-picture really helps the thought and does not hinder it, we are far better without it. If it lures the minds of the listeners away from the truth, we must cut it out and cast it from us. "Our figures," as Spurgeon remarks, "are meant not so much to be seen as to be seen through." Stained-glass windows are all very well in their way, but they are not the kind of windows one would put in a hothouse. They tint the light, but they also stint the light. As William Burkitt long ago expressed it: "Painted glass is very beautiful; but plain glass is the more useful, as it lets through more light." Let us make our sermons, then, richly colorful with brilliant illustrations; but let us not allow the illustrations to attract so much attention to themselves that they deflect the minds of our hearers from the subject on hand.

Yet another snare awaits our unwary feet in this connection— *that of bringing a second-rate illustration into a sermon with an inflated buildup*, as if one should introduce a piccolo solo with a flourish of trumpets. Always we should see to it that any

174

claims we make on behalf of an illustration we mean to use can be justified by the facts. Flattering comments can sometimes have flattening consequences. "Distinguished guests," declares A. J. Gordon, "we may introduce with as extended formality as we choose, but we do not introduce our servants. . . . Illustrations are the preacher's servants. Their elaborate presentation to an audience tends to lift them out of their proper subordination, as though they came to be ministered unto instead of to minister." Never, by anything we say in advance about an anecdote we intend to insert in a sermon, should we arouse in the congregation pleasurable anticipations which we are not able to gratify. Never should we lead our people up the garden path merely to show them out of the back gate. If we do, we shall forfeit their confidence and undermine their respect for our power of discrimination.

An error into which we are especially liable to fall is that of *italicizing the capital "I."* To be sure, there is, as we have seen, a legitimate place in preaching for the ego. Speaking in the pulpit impersonally, we surrender a major element of our power. "In your preaching," counsels Frank Cairns, "don't attempt to hide the fact that you are a human being."

Some years ago there appeared in the popular press a cartoon in which a frustrated-looking man was shown sitting at a vintage-model typewriter. Manifestly he had been making a bid to write a book. Around him were stacked reams of paper, and the wastebasket was positively bulging with discarded sheets. Underneath the sketch were the words: "It's no good. I can't write my autobiography on this machine. The capital 'I' is missing!"

Perhaps, as some think, the tendency of ministers of the Word to refer to themselves in the pulpit is less common nowadays than once it was. It is a mark of the beautiful modesty of the greatest of our Scottish preachers, James S. Stewart, that Horton Davies, after studying Stewart's two masterly volumes of sermons, could "recall only three personal experiences to which he refers." That

THE ART OF ILLUSTRATING SERMONS

is in line with our Lord's own example. John Oman has noted that Jesus "never produces one of His experiences as an illustration."

Alas, it is not always modesty which is today responsible for such pulpit reticence. "One of the most effective ways of illustrating religious reality," observes B. T. Roberts, "is from your own experience. I know this has nearly gone out of fashion. The reason is, not that we have so much humility, but that we have so little experience!"

Nevertheless, the prevailing tendency among modern preachers is probably not to speak too little but to speak too much about themselves. We are all tempted shamefully to overwork that slim slave of a letter—the capital "I." "There are preachers," comments Phillips Brooks, "to whom one could listen for a year, and then he could write their biography, if it were worth the doing. Every truth they wish to teach is illustrated by some event in their own history. Every change of character which they wish to urge is set forth under the form in which that change took place in themselves."

All the same, it would clearly be going too far to infer from this that we are to preach as if we were disembodied spirits to whom nothing had ever happened on this homely earth. One recollects how Emerson referred with scorching scorn to a preacher of that type to whom he listened one snowy Sunday morning and who, for aught he had to say that day, might just as well never have lived in this workaday world at all. We remember likewise Newman's dogmatic dictum: "What is anonymous won't preach."

If our ministry is to sit close to life, if our people are to hear the heartbeat in it, we shall have to put something of ourselves into it. And surely, as someone has sanely said, "modesty is not inconsistent with an appeal to a man's own experience."

Between the two extremes—that of advertising oneself and

that of liquidating oneself—there is a happy medium, and it is at this that we should aim. We are not to be exhibitionists, but equally we are not to be nonentities. The truth is, there are two ways of using the perpendicular pronoun: One is to employ it in the manner of an eyewitness in a court of law, in which case it at once attracts attention and arouses interest; the other is to employ it after the fashion of the boring braggart who repeats it as if it were the only letter in the alphabet, in which case it calls forth nothing but revulsion and disgust.

"I, yet not I" is the central paradox of genuine Christian preaching. As Carl S. Patton incisively put it: "There is an impersonal use of 'I,' in which people see at once that the preacher refers to himself not because he wishes to talk about himself, but because he knows himself better than he knows anyone else."

In the vocabulary of the minister of the Word there should certainly be a letter "I," but it should definitely not be the first letter; Christ must always be the Alpha of his message.

Another homiletic indiscretion we should bypass if we can— that of using without due caution illustrations drawn from realms concerning which listeners are likely to be better informed than ourselves. This is a point W. B. Selbie was wont to press. "Shun fishing illustrations," he urged his students, "when you're near the sea, or agricultural illustrations in farming country."

But surely that was a counsel of despair. For where, after all, are fishing illustrations more certain to be fully apprehended and appreciated than at the seaside, or where can agricultural illustrations be counted upon to meet with a more favorable and encouraging reception than in rural areas? Evidently the Master thought so, when long ago he addressed the fisherfolk and farmers of Galilee in parables suggested by the ways of life they led.

The point that needs to be watched is not to employ such illustrations in such settings without being absolutely sure of one's facts. Failure to do this may betray us into a display of ignorance

177

similar to that of the "Reverend Doctor" of whom Thomas Guthrie tells in his *Autobiography:*

The doctor had gone to preach in Glenisla and, recollecting that that was a pastoral district, he judged that the twenty-third Psalm would be a suitable subject and from that he delivered an admirable discourse. But, in the course of his address, he used an illustration which lowered him in the eyes of the congregation. Unaware of the fact that sheep, in the moist climate and amongst the dew-covered and green succulent herbage of Scotland, are independent of springs, and indeed seldom drink water except when they are sick, he expatiated on the importance of the still waters to the flocks—a blunder and betrayal of ignorance soon noticed by his hearers. As some of them lingered by the church door after the service, the doctor had the mortification of hearing himself and his sermon treated with undisguised contempt, one shepherd saying to another, "Puir bodie! Heard ye ever the like o' yon aboot the sheep drinkin'?" [2]

A similar situation once arose after a sermon by Mark Guy Pearse delivered before a Cornish congregation. Preaching on "Take my yoke upon you, and learn of me" (Matt. 11:29), he explained how smoothly polished and perfectly balanced the yokes were which Jesus made in the carpenter shop at Nazareth. At the close an old farmer took the preacher to task for his ignorance about yokes. "A yoke," he pointed out, "is always heavier at one end than at the other, for no two animals pull with the same strength. The reason why the Master's yoke is light for us is that the heavier end rests on Him."

Nor was the position different with the preacher of whom Frederick A. Farley tells.

In the early days of the motor-car [he] tried to illustrate conversion by pointing out that it was better to turn a car round and face in the opposite direction if it was found that a wrong direction had been taken, than to drive the car very far backwards. The illustra-

---

[2] (London: Daldy, Isbister & Co., 1877), pp. 86-87.

tion might have served very well if he had not used language which betrayed his ignorance. He spoke of "reversing the engine," and a motor-engineer pointed out to him afterwards that an engine is never reversed. It continues to operate in the same way, only it is connected with a gear which drives the car in the reverse direction.[3]

So let us beware of the specialists. Instead of running the risk I have described, let us, before employing a sermon-picture, about the details of which we are in some dubiety, put to a knowledgable person a few discreet, strategic questions. That should elicit all the specialized information we require and we may safely go ahead.

We must, moreover, be wisely careful *not to press the point of an illustration too far.* All sorts of mischief proliferate from this malpractice. No doubt it was a recognition of this which led Luther to maintain that "metaphors are a soil very productive of heresies." Every well-built word-picture is designed to do one thing and one thing only. So long as it fulfills that function and illuminates some specific aspect of truth, experience, or duty, it is doing its job and should not be expected to do anything else. "If an illustration will go with you a mile," says Spurgeon, "do not compel it to go with you twain." To the same purpose is the following quaint prayer of Thomas Fuller: "Grant, O Lord, that I may never rack a Scripture simile beyond the true intent thereof, lest instead of sucking milk I squeeze blood out of it."

We should always respect the limits of the illustrations we employ, driving home as with a hammerblow the particular point we want to press, but not hitting so hard as to split the board. To vary the figure, the beam will be all the brighter and more penetrative for being focused.

Another common mistake now merits brief mention—*that of using an illustration which itself needs illustrating.* The lamp that burns so feebly that one has to light another lamp to see it is a pitifully poor illuminant. Very different are the exquisite

[3] *Preparing to Preach* (London: Epworth Press, 1939), pp. 36-37.

word-pictures painted by our Lord. None of them requires any clarification whatever in order to be readily grasped by the simplest mind. Every one of them is not only self-explanatory but provides a luminous commentary on the meaning of the truth on which Jesus wishes to train the spiritual spotlight or the imperative importance of the moral obligation which he desires to lay upon the conscience of his listeners. Under this head T. De Witt Talmage has some pertinent observations: "Christ's illustrations were drawn from everyday life. We hardly ever hear Him making any allusion to any Grecian or Egyptian antiquities. . . . His comparisons are as plain as that white is white and black is black, and the most illiterate man that ever heard Jesus talk knew immediately what He meant."

In this as in all else the Master is our supreme model. The illustrations of certain modern preachers remind us of contemporary art, which is supposed to interpret some facet of nature or of human life, but which is itself far more baffling and bewildering than any of its subjects. Of Robert Rainy a wag once said that occasionally in his preaching he was not only rainy but misty. In a sermon an illustration is meant to shine like a ray of sunlight, banishing mental mist; but if the illustration itself is cloudy, it will only make obscurity doubly obscure.

Closely analogous is the next caution to which we should pay heed, a caution often expressed in the maxim: *"Don't labor the moral."* That there are lessons to be drawn from the stories we tell in the pulpit goes without saying, otherwise to offer them there would be irrelevant and a sheer waste of time. But, though the lessons are to be drawn, we must not let them be too long-drawn-out. We recall the preference confessed to by the little girl and also her reason for it: "I do like our minister. He's got no morals!" We remember, too, how once Robertson of Irvine, Scotland (a great man in his day, though not so famous as his namesake of Brighton), addressing a crowd of children in Glasgow, held their close attention by his stories until he felt it was time to bring things to a point. "Now this teaches us, . . ."

he began. But he was rudely interrupted. "Never mind what it teaches," broke out a boy on the front seat, "gie's anither story!" "I learned from that rascal," says Robertson, "to wrap the moral well in the heart of the story, not to put it as a sting into the tail. For stories are like pictures, and their lessons should be felt but never obtruded." "The image," wrote John Oman, "should incarnate the thought and not merely illustrate it." G. K. Chesterton expressed the same thing neatly when he said: "A good story does not *have* a moral, it *is* a moral." The instruction to be derived from the word-picture should be embodied and embedded, wherever possible, in the illustration itself, as the barb is in the bait.

Where this cannot be done, brevity, pungency, and directness are prime prerequisites to the effective application of illustrations. As Henry Sloane Coffin has contended: "Laboured applications are boresome, for they are swiftly caught by listeners and lose in power when expanded. If they really are good word-pictures, we shall not need to elaborate them, especially in the case of those dealing with moral questions." Boswell once said of Johnson that in the cut and thrust of debate, he wasted no time in brandishing his sword but "was through your body in an instant." Similar dispatch should in preaching characterize the applying of illustrations. "In the surgery of the conscience," counseled Paxton Hood, "do not use chloroform, and let the operation be brief."

The last trap to be dodged is that of *falsifying by exuberant fancy what we expect our hearers to accept as fact*. We have all laughed at the tale of the little lass whose father was a minister and who, at dinner in the manse, after the good man had regaled his guests with the latest addition to his anecdotal repertoire, innocently inquired: "Is that true, Daddy, or are you only preaching?" For some of us that story contains a necessary caution. How easy it is for us unconsciously to embroider a tale, adding a touch here and there, until when we have told it a score of times, it has probably grown and altered beyond all recognition. The artist in us unconsciously polishes the facts even if

181

the egoist in us is too honest deliberately to tamper with them. Nor does the egoist always have such scruples. Some pulpit speakers, it is said, do not hesitate to add spice to a borrowed narrative by purposely setting themselves at the center of it. This is a species of dishonesty in which it is not only despicable but dangerous to indulge. Spurgeon once caught an unlucky clergyman at it. The fellow claimed that a certain happening had just befallen him, when Spurgeon had reported it of himself more than twenty years before.

To be quite fair, however, such conscious deception is probably practiced very rarely indeed in the pulpit. Usually there is no desire or design to deceive. In fact, many of us, if surprised in the act of spinning a specious yarn, would hotly resent any suggestion that it was spurious and contend vehemently for its literal truth. Having retailed the unconsciously garbled version so often, we have come to believe it ourselves. That is a foible against which we must maintain a constant watch.

Such, then, are the pictorial pitfalls that beset the preacher's path. In the face of them we may well make John Henry Newman's prayer our own: "Keep Thou my feet."

7

Putting Them Across

People sometimes try to sum up a whole age in a single phrase. It is a rather risky thing to do, and yet there would seem to be some truth and descriptive value in such rough generalizations. Men speak of "The Age of Faith," "The Age of Reason," "The Age of Industrial Revolution," and so on. And, when they talk so, all informed persons know at once to which periods of history they are referring.

If asked thus to put a label on our own age, what should we say? How should we describe it? Several apt epithets immediately spring to mind, for ours is a complex and many-faceted generation. It can, as we have noted in the first chapter, most fittingly be called "The Age of Illustration"; but it might be better to broaden that title a bit and term ours "The Age of Communication." For nothing is more typical of our time than the invention, production, and use of techniques and media of verbal transmission.

In such a day surely it should not be difficult for us to realize how crucially important in preaching is the art of putting things across. Never should we forget that our task, as compared, say, with that of the author or journalist, is doubly arduous and exacting. All they have to do is to express themselves—as cogently, colorfully, and convincingly as they can—on paper. Once they have committed their ideas to writing in the finest and fittest language at their command, their work is finished. With us it is otherwise. When we have reached that stage in the preparation of our sermons, we have still a long way to go. We have still to give them oral expression, still to project them past the Paper Curtain, still to get them over.

Charles James Blomfield was wont to tell his students: "A sermon is no good unless you can get it across." That would appear to be self-evident, and yet how often it is overlooked! Not one preacher in ten pays sufficient attention to the delivery of his discourses. The theory seems to be that, provided pains are taken to make the sermon as nearly perfect as possible in the study, the matter of putting it over can be more or less left to look after itself. Nothing could be further from the truth. Doubtless, as Gene E. Bartlett has reminded us, our primary duty is not to deliver sermons but to deliver souls, yet the tragic fact is that souls in urgent need of deliverance may never be delivered because we do not know how to deliver our sermons. A poor sermon demands a good delivery; a fine sermon deserves one. And we should be very foolish indeed were we to underestimate or to neglect the vital question of presentation.

To no part of preaching does this apply more peremptorily than to that of illustration. "A good story ill told is a bad one," says the proverb. For the painter to complete his canvas in the privacy of his studio is one thing, but it is not everything. Art presupposes a viewer as well as a painter. The artist has still to exhibit his work; and it is not the effect it has on himself in the studio but the impression it makes on the public at the exhibition which finally signifies.

So with sermon illustrating. In the study our word-pictures may appear to us admirably adapted to illuminate some aspect of life or thought or faith, but that is not the point. The point is: What do our people think of them? Do they see them in sharp focus and true perspective, or do our illustrations seem to them blurred, hazy, indistinct? In other words, do we, or do we not, succeed in putting them across?

That so many of the homiletic experts should have stressed this question was only to be expected. "Every preacher," wrote John Kelman, "should give earnest attention and deliberate study to the art of telling a story. It is a thing which everybody supposes himself able to do, and which surprisingly few can really do well." More recently Ronald A. Ward has struck the same note. He says: "Study the techniques of story-telling."

This is the subject which we come now to discuss. Perhaps we can best handle it under the following four headings.

First, let us consider the *place* where they are to be put across.

To be employed to most advantage, illustrations must be adapted to the age in which they are given, to the personality of the preacher, to the character of the sermon, and to the nature of the building in which they are to be delivered.

A small matter this last may be, but it is a matter nonetheless about which something must be said. Before giving an illustration it is wise to take into account the type of place in which it is to be presented. An anecdote which would be perfectly in order in one church might be utterly out of keeping in another.

Not all places of worship are suited to the telling of stories in the pulpit. Indeed, some would appear almost to have been planned and built of set purpose to frustrate any such attempt. There are ecclesiastical edifices in which it would be well-nigh impossible to employ a kindling illustration—gloomy, sepulchral, half-lit, draughty caves, in which the only sort of ministry consonant with the surroundings would be a raven-like croaking about human mortality! Happily, there are other sanctuaries which are highly conducive to a pictorial mode of preaching and in which it is a pleasure to illuminate one's message with living word-pictures.

To be sure, if a preacher is not sensitive to atmosphere he will not be unduly influenced by artchitecture. Some are so impervious to impressions of this kind that they would crack a joke in a funeral parlor! Most of us, fortunately, are not as crass as that. To a larger extent than we commonly realize our preaching is modified and conditioned by its material setting.

In any case, it is politic to see to it that, as far as may be, our illustrations harmonize with the nature of the place in which they are presented. Artists, as we all know, fall into various categories and specialize in different branches of art. Some, like William Blake, excel in etching; others, like Russell Flint, in watercolors; others, again, like William Joseph Turner, in oils. Each selects the art form most expressive of his genius and best fitted to embody his purpose. Similarly preachers have their own favorite types of illustration, and it is desirable that the nature of the illustration should accord with that of the building in which it is to be delivered. Every picture—oil painting, water color, life-sized portait, miniature, or what have you—must be suitably displayed. A pen-and-ink sketch, however exquisite as a work of art, would look more than odd—if in truth it could be seen at all—on the ceiling of the Sistine Chapel, and the mighty frescoes of Michelangelo would seem curiously incongruous on the wall of a downtown mission hall.

Just so with illustrations. They should never be in clashing contrast to the character of the church in which they are to be given. When planning their presentation we cannot afford to ignore the place in which they are to be delivered.

Secondly, we should look at the *people* to whom they are to be put across.

To us as sermon-artists our hearers are both canvas and patrons, at once the materials on which our paintings are executed, and the public who inspect and appraise them. Hence for a double reason the people deserve our close concern. "Ever remember," said Matthew Simpson, "that God sends people to hear you as well as you to preach." "There is a man," as Donald Macleod has it, "at both ends of the sermon." And Thomas H. Keir reasonably enough remarks that it is possible to reverse Paul's query, "How shall they hear without a preacher?" and to ask, "How shall they preach without a hearer?" The one is as essential as the other. This recollection and reflection must always be regulative in this whole business of making and giving illustrations.

There are two strikingly impressive testimonies which ought to be inscribed in letters of gold on the wall of some room in every church. They are the utterances of two famous preachers of our time, representative of widely different schools of theological thought, and they are companion pictures, complementary to each other. The first is by Frank W. Boreham. "I have never entered a pulpit," he confesses, "without feeling that, if only the people can catch a vision of the Saviour, they would have no alternative but to lay their devotion at His feet." The other is by Harry Emerson Fosdick. "I know what I want to say to myself before anything else when I get into the pulpit," he declares. "There is in that congregation one person who needs what I am going to say. Oh, God, let me get at him!" Truly, as Gene E. Bartlett has neatly told us: "The pew is one place where the ultimate and the intimate meet." And we must never suffer to fade from our minds the thrilling thought that some illustration of ours may prove the point of contact between them.

Prior to preaching, we need to keep our prospective congregation clearly in view and adjust the illustrative content of our sermon accordingly.

For one thing, we need to take some notice of the probable size of the congregation. Obviously, we cannot preach to two thousand as we would to twenty. The crowd calls for a different technique. To grasp and grapple with a great audience, we have to throw ourselves into the delivery of a discourse far more than would be necessary to secure similar results with a smaller gathering. This has its bearing on our means of offering our illustrations.

Perhaps, though, it is not so much the actual size of the congregation itself as its size in proportion to the place it occupies which mainly matters. Of this every practiced speaker is well aware. Henry Ward Beecher once claimed that he could undertake to electrify the biggest audience provided its members sat close together, but put them all four feet apart and he was done for! "I had rather," averred T. De Witt Talmage, "preach in a full barn than in a sparsely-attended cathedral"—a perfectly understandable preference. Before presenting our word-pictures we should endeavor to assess the size of the gathering in which they are to be given. Numbering the people in this manner is not the sin of arithmetic which King David committed; it is the essential precondition of getting illustrations across.

For another thing, we ought to reckon with the mentality of the congregation. The old orators were wont to talk of what they called "the law of accommodation," in accordance with which the public speaker was to descend and condescend to his audience, to get down to their level so as to lift them up to his.

That is a principle on which the great popular preachers of history uniformly proceeded. Luther, as is well known, confessed that if, when about to deliver a discourse, he observed among his listeners men of light and learning, he was sometimes tempted to direct his message to them, as he could so well have done, on their own intellectual plane. But recollecting that if he so spoke he would not be understood by the poor, ignorant, illiterate multitude, he resolutely set the temptation aside and adopted a simple and homely style of address, assured that by so doing he would make his meaning manifest to all. John Wesley, as we have already noted, was of the same mind. "I design plain speech for plain people," he affirmed. And Joseph Parker in his overmastering concern thus mentally to identify himself with the members of his congregation could actually declare in that dramatic way of his: "I am one of my listeners!" All of these preachers would have subscribed without reservation to the sentiment expressed by Augustine: "I had rather that the grammarians found fault with me than that the people should misunderstand me." Comprehension is crucial. If our hearers do not follow us, it is just as if we were talking to them in a foreign tongue. We may *think* like the scholar in the university, but in the pulpit we must *speak* like the man in the street. If we are wise, we shall always hang our pictures at eye-level.

At this juncture it may be pertinent to interject a few comments on the children's address—so often little more than an extended illustration—which by a custom as rigid and inflexible as the laws of the Medes and Persians is incorporated in the public worship of many modern churches. And here let me say outright that some preachers are constitutionally incapable of giving a children's address, and that it is a pity that the unwelcome duty is thrust upon them, for often the thing is so badly done that it spoils the rest of the service which may be of a very high standard.

Of course, there is another side to this. Some preachers have a happy knack of delivering children's addresses—and can deliver nothing else! In this connection one recalls Dr. Gossip's famous story of how once in Edinburgh that superb pulpit stylist, W. M. Macgregor, was taken to hear a much-vaunted "star" preacher. The sermon was just a series of stories loosely strung together on a thin thread of thought, and Macgregor was not at all impressed. On the way home, his friend dared not broach the subject for fear of an outburst, and so for awhile the two strode along in silence. Presently, however, Macgregor's companion did venture the remark: "Well, anyhow, it was a nice children's address that he gave." "Two children's addresses," growled Macgregor.

For all that, the impressive delivery of a children's address is by no means to be despised. It is in fact one of the pulpit's rarest accomplishments. With regard to it two pitfalls have to be avoided. The first is that of speaking to the little folk in a stilted and patronizing tone, talking down to them, as we say, as if from the top of a tall pedestal. The second is that of speaking to them from below the mental level of the youngest of them, as if one were addressing them from underneath the floorboards. Really to reach them, we must be neither above nor below them, but on their plane. And we must actually talk to them and not just in their presence.

In point of fact, there are two ways of presenting a children's address. One is to offer it to the adults in the audience in the hope that the children will overhear it; the other is, for the time being, to forget all about the grown-ups and to give it to the youngsters as if they alone were in the church. It is easy to see which of these methods is the better. Where the presentation of the children's address is concerned, the "law of accommodation" must come into operation if the thing is to be done well.

Returning to the matter of adjusting illustrations to the mentality of mature congregations, it may not be without interest to remark that some preachers have so excelled in this direction that they have actually been able to extemporize word-pictures while standing up before the people, devising one illustration after another because they saw each fitted particularly some member of the audience. That, as we colloquially express it, "takes some doing." None but the experienced, not to say the expert, need attempt it with any expectation of success.

Henry Ward Beecher tells us that now and then he tried his hand at it, and if we were all Henry Ward Beechers we might do the same. He writes:

I may suggest that it is a good thing in looking over an audience, to cultivate the habit of seeing illustrations in them. If I see a seaman sitting among my audience, I do not say, "I will use him as a figure," and apply it personally; but out of him jumps an illustration from the sea, and it comes to seek me out. If there be a watchmaker present, that I happen to recognize, my next illustration will very likely be from horology—though he will be utterly unconscious of the fact that I have used him. Then I see a schoolmistress, and my next illustration will be out of schoolteaching. Thus, where your audience is known to you, the illustration ought not simply to meet

190

your wants as a speaker, but should meet the wants of your congregation. It should be a help to them.[1]

All of which just serves to show that genius cannot be trusted when it tries to legislate for ordinary individuals. If, as I said, we were all Henry Ward Beechers, that advice would be worth taking; and the practice it recommends would, if adopted, add immeasurably to the effectiveness of the pictorial element in our preaching. But we are not Henry Ward Beechers and never shall be Henry Ward Beechers; and, so far as we are concerned, the counsel, capital as it would be in other circumstances, is a counsel of perfection which must be treated with the greatest of caution and reserve.

To say this is not to deny that, if we are to deliver them effectively, our illustrations must be characterized by a certain amount of elasticity. They must be capable within limits, of adaptation to immediate requirements and conditions. Earlier in these pages we have reminded ourselves that the word-picture as written may be, and indeed should be, set down in fixed and final form, but that the word-picture as delivered must be left, as far as possible, flexible and fluid, so that it can be tailored to the precise needs of some specific congregation. Time, circumstances, and aim may determine whether in its delivery an illustration should be packed into a phrase and presented in the form of metaphor, whether it should assume the character of a similitude running to two or three sentences, or whether its dimensions may profitably be expanded to those of a full-length story or parable.

There is, of course, a difference, which should be obvious, between extending in the pulpit an illustration which we have thought out fully in the study and extemporizing an illustration which we have not thought out at all!

"The adroit use of illustrations," remarks David Williamson,

[1] *Popular Lectures on Preaching* (London: Simpkin, Marshall & Co., 1872), p. 138.

"calls for brevity and succinctness in relating an incident." Of the written illustration that is certainly true; but, as regards the spoken illustration, the statement requires qualifying. Several things may determine the length of the story as told. The more complex and complicated it is, the more sides it has, the more involved and intricate its detail, the longer it will take in the telling and the harder it will be to unravel in public without losing the listeners' interest.

Speaking generally, the slow and labored start is not to be commended. While we are setting the table, the appetite of our guests abates. But there are times when a laggardly introduction is justifiable, perhaps even essential. We must give our people time to "tune in" their minds to our illustrative wavelength. It is of no use starting to unfold the narrative until they are thoroughly "with us." Embarking too briskly on the telling of the tale, we may find to our chagrin that our hearers' full attention and appreciation have been awakened too late for them to grasp its meaning or to catch its point. Better is it to "angle" for their interest for awhile and not to draw in the line until we are quite sure that they have risen to our bait and got hooked on our barb. When the congregation is alive, alert, alight, we may sketch in a word-painting with a few swift strokes; but when the audience is slow, sluggish, lethargic, indifferent, we may need to "play" with it as an angler plays with a big salmon, waiting for a bite. We shall have to learn what that word meaneth: "Tell me the story slowly, that I may take it in." Such was the sagacious strategy of Rowland Hill. "They say I ramble," he remarked to his congregation one day, "but it is because you ramble, and I am obliged to ramble after you."

Woe to us, however, if we ramble too far! There is, as we have seen, a grave peril in extemporizing the delivery of an illustration. It may carry us whither we would not.

Anyhow, we shall have to weigh up the mentality of our hearers and make whatever adjustments are necessary to our word-pictures accordingly. "Illustrations, to be of real help," remarks

Robert R. Resker, "must be within the compass of the knowledge or experience of those to whom they are addressed."

For yet a further thing, we shall require to measure the mood of our congregation. Congregations do have moods—good moods and bad—but precisely why they have them is by no means easy to ascertain. All sorts of things probably combine to produce them—the season of the year, the time of day, the political situation, the condition of trade, the atmosphere of the church, the presence of the preacher—each contributes its own quota in one way or another, not to mention infinitely more important factors such as the moral and spiritual background of the people's lives.

Audiences vary extraordinarily in emotional response and even in emotional potential; and, on the whole, the more susceptible they are to emotion the likelier they are to be either the best or the worst of congregations. In an expansive, ebullient, jubilant mood such an audience will almost put words in a speaker's mouth; in a bad mood, it will defy Demosthenes himself to rouse it.

Nor is this all. Not only do different congregations vary in emotional response, the same congregation may vary very considerably in the course of a single service. Therein lies our hope. With the help of God we may change the mood. Naturally, the theme which we happen to be handling at the time will dictate our own mood to a large degree; and, if we know our business as preachers, our mood will dictate that of the congregation.

Never should we with supine fatalism accept the fact that at the commencement of a service the congregation is dull and listless. Rather should we make up our minds that it shall not long continue thus. Of John Hunter it was said that he possessed the rare art of carrying the feelings of his people with him from point to point of the sermon, gearing them in to his growing thought from first to last. That is truly a notable achievement, not fully within the range of our more modest powers. Yet we

193

need not just resign ourselves to what we judge to be the inevitable. We need not merely "prose on while they doze on." God assisting us, we can do much to alter the situation.

Startlingly unexpected was the rejoinder of Henry Ward Beecher when asked by the minister of a rural church how to stop hardworking farmers from going to sleep during the sermon. "In our church," replied Beecher, "we have had for years an able-bodied committee whose duty it is when anyone is discovered asleep in the congregation to go into the pulpit and wake up the pastor!"

Yes, we can do something about it, and we ought to do something about it. To be sure, torpor in a congregation at the start of a religious service is not the preacher's fault (although it may have an oblique relation to him, indicating that he is not the sort of speaker from whom the people look for very much); but torpor in the middle or at the end of a service most definitely is the preacher's fault and is a clear sign that he is not up to his job.

There is an allusion in one of Adolf Deissmann's books to "the excellent Eutychus, whose name is a warning to all who slumber in church and who was certainly one of the extremely few people who managed to go to sleep in the presence of St. Paul." Spotting among our congregation "that noisome pestilence, the person whose nod is not that of assent but of somnolence," we had better take prompt steps to wake him up as soon as possible, and one of the best ways of doing so will be to make absolutely certain that we are wide awake ourselves.

Thus shall we master the mood of our congregation and ever, as the mood changes, we shall be ready to introduce into our methods of delivering illustrations any modifications which we consider necessary or desirable.

Thirdly, we must think of the *person by whom* they are to be put across.

Here we come to the artist himself, the man who is to do the illustrating. In other words, we look in the mirror. And, of course, in every case the quality of the painting we produce will be an exact index of the quality of the painter. The artist, it is said, cannot help painting himself. That is certainly true of the sermon artist. You will remember Leonardo da Vinci's self-revealing lament: "If I had been a better man, I should have painted a better picture." However that may have applied to da Vinci, it most assuredly applies to the sermon illustrator. Whatever else in our preaching we deliver or fail to deliver, we shall always get our own picture over. Of Phillips Brooks it was said that he was "a walking illustration of the truth he taught."

If, then, we are to put our illustrations across with maximum effect, what must we do by way of preparation for the effort?

We must see to it, as far as we can, that our bodies are at their best. Some preachers of scholarly cast remind me of what Yehudi Menuhin would be like trying to woo soul-melting music out of a worm-eaten and broken-backed violin. The talent —almost amounting, in certain cases, to genius—is there, but the instrument is defective through sheer ill-usage. Is that not a tragedy? For what does it profit a preacher to have a brilliant brain, stocked with as much miscellaneous knowledge as an encyclopedia, if his body is such a wreck that it cannot get his message over? If there is one thing that a lifetime in the ministry teaches us, it is this: So strictly does God respect his own laws of health that he will not suspend them even in favor of a man who overspends his energies in the sacred service. "What we sow we reap" applies even here.

Nor is this all. So often in such circumstances the physical affects the psychological with calamitous consequences. A preacher in that overwrought state will sometimes solemnly tell us that he has committed the unpardonable sin, when we know very well that the only unpardonable sin he has committed is that of grossly neglecting and overtaxing his body. Simple things such as diet, rest, and exercise have far more to do with the effective delivery of sermons than they are commonly given credit for, even by those whose task it is to compose the sermons. Never should we, of all people, underestimate the significance

195

of physical factors in the ministry, remembering that it is for us a religious duty to look after our bodies.

The mind, too, if it is to function at its finest in the ministry, must be accorded a proper care. Negatively, it must be kept free from anxiety, and positively it must be soaked in its message, as the dyer's hand takes on the color of the stuff in which it works. To the impressive presentation of illustrations in particular two things are essential; the preacher must have nothing on his mind and he must have something in his mind. The one is almost as necessary as the other. To me an artist friend once said: "I always paint best when I am happy." One understands that. As Matthew Arnold expressed it in his "Caution to Poets":

> What poets feel not, when they make,
> A pleasure in creating,
> The world, in *its* turn, will not take
> Pleasure in contemplating.

But that is only one aspect of the matter. The other is that, before preaching, our thoughts ought to be impregnated both with each illustration itself and with the truth it is designed to illuminate. Arthur T. Pierson once said: "Without much meditation, reading is like eating that which you do not digest"; and Charles Reynolds Brown prescribes the remedy for such failure in mental digestion: "Brood over your material until you are fully in the mood of your message."

The artist sees three pictures for every one he paints—the picture in his mind before he sets to work on the canvas, the picture he actually puts on the canvas, and the mental picture of it he afterward carries about with him everywhere he goes. We likewise must have in our minds before entering the pulpit a lucid perception of every word-painting we intend to use, it must be clear to us while we are actually giving it, and it must be luminous in the recollection of our listeners long after its delivery.

Not only must we prepare our bodies and minds for putting our illustrations over, however, we must also pay attention to

196

our spirits. Nobody would ever dream of telling a story in private conversation to anyone he disliked or to whom he was utterly indifferent; and no man in the pulpit ever presented a word-picture effectively if he was out of harmony with his hearers. Good relations, if one may so express it, are indispensable to good narrations. If there is even one person in the congregation with whom we are not on speaking terms, we had better not try to get illustrations across, for unless our lives illustrate our message we shall never be able to illustrate it in any other way. When Frank Leighton was president of the Royal Academy he made this striking statement: "No error is deeper or more deadly than the denial that the moral complexion, the ethos, of the artist does in truth tinge every work of his hand, and fashion—in silence, but with the certainty of fate—the course and current of his whole career."

The older one grows in the ministry, the more impressed does one become with the absolute necessity to effective preaching, especially to effective pictorial preaching, of harmonious personal relations between the minister and the members of his congregation; and that means not only abstention from wrong relations with them but the discharge to the best of his ability of his high responsibilities toward them.

Above all, if we are to put our illustrations across successfully, we must be in vital touch with the Spirit of God. Without that, we shall have no inspiration, and what is an artist of any kind without inspiration? The man who paints carriages can go about his job in cold blood, but the man who paints canvases must wait till his heart waxes warm within him. Lacking the afflatus, the finest artist is but a poor dauber. He may be able to apply colors to his board, but he cannot impart life to his pictures.

So with us in connection with our word-paintings. Wanting the Holy Spirit, we want all. For what are our ingenious schemes for discovering, devising, storing, and delivering illustrations but an elaborate futility unless he is with us in the work? Describing a discourse he had heard, W. H. H. Murray passed on it this caustic comment: "The sermon was verbally exact; it was suggestive; it was ornate: but, alas, something was missing. That something was God." Could any criticism have been more utterly annihilating? We may be sure of this; no preacher can prepare and present living word-pictures, vividly illuminative of eternal realities, without the aid of the blessed Spiirt, any more than Raphael and Rubens, for all their natural gifts, could have painted their masterpieces without inspiration. A brilliant brain, a soaring imagination, the lordship of language, even if one had such things, would not suffice. Lacking the breath divine, the best of us lie inert and motionless like a barque becalmed. To get our illustrations tellingly over, we must be inspired. That means prayer, study, meditation, a disciplined and holy life. Yet in the end it is God's gift. We cannot win it or work for it; we must await its coming as the old mariners waited for wind.

Lastly, consider the process by which they are to be put across.

By way of background preparation for this, there is one thing we may do which will materially aid us in presenting our illustrations. We may try out our stories in private conversation with our friends prior to giving them in the pulpit. Only, we must make sure that the stories are of the sort which can be counted on to appeal to those to whom we propose to retail them, that our friends are in the mood and have the time to listen to them, that we do not repeat the stories to the same people, and, before all else, that we do not convey to our hearers the impression that we are using them as homiletic guinea pigs. Having satisfied ourselves on these particulars, we may go ahead with our narration, painting in the scene, describing the action, reporting the dialogue in such wise as to bring things to a climax and elicit the desired response. There is nothing to prevent our telling the tale over and over again to different sets of persons; and always, as we tell it, we may touch it up here and there, cutting out a redundant phrase at this point and adding a depictive sentence at that, accelerating or slackening the tempo, and so on; until, by and by, we reach a stage at which we feel that we cannot improve on our performance. Such a practice, if persisted in, will help us much in putting our illustrations over.

Having said this much about modes of presenting illustrations, let us move forward to discuss further matters of vital relevance to their telling delivery.

Of these the first matter concerns posture, stance, manner. And here the ideal to aim at is naturalness. But it must be, if the phrase is allowable, a cultivated naturalness, the naturalness of one to whom art has become second nature. Of one preacher it was said that "he was as much at home in the pulpit as if he had been born in it." But what is a "natural" manner in the pulpit? Presumably, it will differ somewhat in every instance in accordance with variations in individuality. Broadly speaking, however, we can confidently state that it will be marked by avoidance of two extremes—a soldierly stiffness and a gelatinous slouchiness.

Looking down from the sacred desk some men become like Lot's wife when she looked back on Sodom—petrified. Not so much with fear as with formalism. They may still be the salt of the earth, but it is a pity they assume the shape of a pillar. Anyhow, one thing is certain; no such crystallized cleric will ever succeed in putting over his illustrations. As well expect a man in a straitjacket to succeed as an acrobat. Of J. H. Jowett, Horton Davies says that his self-command when preaching was almost too faultless. "He seemed at times a rhetorical robot, the perfect imitation of a man—as if interior clockwork had set a Madame Tussaud's waxwork figure in motion." That is one extreme to eschew.

On the other hand, there are preachers who have a sort of india-rubber flaccidity in the pulpit and who drape themselves over the lectern, or lounge against the rail, as if paralyzed from the waist down. A minister I heard in Scotland recently delivered his entire discourse hanging bodily out of the side of the pulpit in the manner of the engineer of a moving train leaning out of

199

THE ART OF ILLUSTRATING SERMONS

his cab. To the hearer it was most exasperating. Slovenly slouch-
ing is the other extreme to be shunned.

To get illustrations across grippingly we need to be flexible but
not flabby, relaxed but not as spineless as a sponge, always remembering that a pompous person can never tell a story well but
that neither can one whose body is not swiftly obedient to his
mind.

At this point it may not be inopportune to introduce a few
observations on practicing what we preach. No, this is not now
meant as a moral maxim. That our lives as preachers should line
up with our message goes without saying. But at the moment we
are thinking rather of the practice of preaching itself, the skill
that comes through drill.

And here we run up against a curious fact. How strangely
shy and self-conscious we preachers are about thus preparing for
the delivery of our sermons. That orators in other branches of
human effort need to do so is taken for granted. We hear of
Demosthenes exercising himself in his art, pebble in mouth,
on the beach; or of Winston Churchill declaiming his polished
periods in the corner of a garden. But somehow there seems to
be something not quite proper in a preacher practicing his art!

Very probably, it is just as well that we feel like that. At the
back of our minds there is—as there certainly should be—a fear,
a perfectly legitimate and wholesome fear, of anything savoring
of artificiality in the ministry of the Word of God. George
Tyrrell once wrote almost savagely: "I can forgive a woman
easily who paints, enamels, and dyes, but a preacher who prac-
tices his sermon before a cheval glass (as some of our French
celebrities do) seems to me farther away from God and reality
than the blackest atheist in existence." Strong words—over-
strong—and yet they are a salutary protest against everything
false and factitious in preparation for the pulpit.

Nevertheless, if we are to get our illustrations across, we shall
have to adopt measures of some kind to master our materials.
This means entering into them mentally and emotionally to such

an extent that our bodies themselves are, as it were, caught up in the process like dust in a desert whirlwind. William Foster-Harris in his *Basic Formulas of Fiction* gives this near-amusing advice to the literary aspirant. "Lock yourself up in a private cell, if you think you must; but do not hesitate to laugh, cry real tears, get furiously angry, or whatever, as your character meets situations evoking these emotions. For when you do, you will find a very strange and cheering thing beginning to happen. The words you write will begin to be charged with story vitality."

Not every sermon illustration is so supercharged with feeling as to call for such dramatic practice as a preliminary to its impressive presentment. Yet the exaggerated instance may serve to direct attention to the importance for our purpose of thus becoming emotionally involved in the unfolding of the narrative.

Actually two errors are to be avoided in this connection. One is that of too much detachment from the illustration, a retailing of it which is coldly dispassionate and unemotional. To relate a story purporting to be full of drama and excitement in a cool and casual fashion is to falsify it by one's way of telling it, for no one who really believed it would ever narrate it in that way. The other error is to overdramatize the tale, acting it as though on the stage, mimicking the movements of the characters, and attempting to imitate the vocal peculiarities in the dialogue. So far from enhancing the effect of the illustration, this gravely detracts from it, making the whole performance offensively theatrical and obviously put on.

Between these two ways of presenting illustrations the line is difficult to draw. Difficult or not, however, drawn it must be. But, if I am compelled to choose the lesser of two evils, I unhesitatingly express my preference for the latter. It is better to put too much emotion into the telling of a story than too little.

Only, the emotion must be real. At all costs we must steer clear of what Sangster aptly styles "faked feeling," the simulation of an empathy which one does not in fact possess. In no part of the delivery of a discourse is the temptation to lapse into such emotional insincerity stronger than in the case of illustrations. The tawdry pretense deceives nobody. People can tell right away when feeling is feigned. They have no trouble whatever in distinguishing between "the taking gift of unction" and its miserable counterfeit, mere unctuousness. We must not be maudlin or melodramatic. The emotion must be real.

Passing from these somewhat general considerations, let us descend to particulars concerning other matters of no less moment in the delivery of illustrations.

The first of these is the voice and its management. It goes without saying that we can no more effectively present our word-pictures without an adequate and suitable vocal apparatus than an artist can execute a masterpiece in oils without paint. And here, of course, natural endowment plays a big part. Not all pulpit voices have the same native quality and even those of recognized excellence are valued for various reasons—clarity, sonority, mellifluousness, and so on. The voice of Charles Haddon Spurgeon was said to be as sweet and clear in tone as a bell; that of Joseph Parker was compared to a cathedral organ in its depth and range and rotundity; that of Leslie Weatherhead has been aptly likened to the mesmeric moan of a violin. Men so dowered have a marvelous advantage in getting illustrations across. Of Robertson of Irvine someone beautifully said: "His voice sounded in my ears like music long remembered." What a gift!

And yet such a voice is not an unmixed blessing. A glorious vocal instrument can be to the preacher a drawback in two directions. It can deflect his own mind from his theme, and it can so enthrall his congregation that they become captivated by it at the expense of the truth it is striving to express. Listening to some men in the ministry, one at once realizes that they enjoy listening to themselves. That, it may be argued, is very natural. So it is, but it is fatal to the effective presentation of a word-picture. For if, when giving the illustration, a man's mind is on his own voice—the purity of its tone, the precision of its elocution, the elegance of its diction, the correctness of its phrasing, and so forth—that is where the listeners' minds are likely to be too; and the story, however fine and finished, may largely be lost in the telling. There will then be a repetition of the experience of Ezekiel: "And, lo, thou art unto them as a very lovely song of one that hath a pleasant voice, and can play well on an instrument: for they hear thy words, but they do them not" (Ezek. 33:32).

That is, of course, one of the hazards of the ministry, a risk we have to take. We are not to try to cultivate ragged, rasping tones for fear that people will get carried away with our vocal perfection. Obviously, the better voice we bring to the delivery of our illustrations the more powerful their effect is likely to be. Nor need we supinely assume that if the organ of speech with which nature has endowed us is of inferior quality, it must of necessity continue so. It is amazing what can be done by expert tuition in elocution, and even, where that is not available, by the persistent self-application of the principles set forth in any worthwhile book on the subject. To name only two little volumes that are worth their weight in gold in this connection, I have myself found very helpful *Manual of Elocution for the Ministry*, by Frank Philip and *Speech in the Pulpit*, by Paul E. Sangster. Anyone studying these works carefully and practicing the simple exercises they prescribe cannot fail to benefit enormously. Almost immediately there will be a perceptible improvement in tonal quality, and the preacher will cease grunting at his hearers like a sow or "talking to them in the key of the cockatoo."

One of the first things to be attended to will be pitch. Experience, if not intuition, teaches us that when we start to tell a story in the pulpit, the most sensible tone to adopt is that of ordinary conversation. Each of us has a natural tone of voice, and it is at that level that we ought to begin. In the unfolding of the narrative there will be points at which we shall want to drop our voices for effect; but, if we are already at rock bottom, how can we further descend? And just as surely there will be points at which we shall wish to lift our voices; but, if we are already at high C, how can we go higher, unless in truth we trill off into a tremulous and unintelligible falsetto? It is therefore wise to give most of the illustration in the middle register of the voice.

But how shall we find our vocal Plimsoll line? A piano can help us here. Speaking at our normal pitch, those of us with any ear for music can go over to the keyboard and at once identify the note. That is our natural level. In telling a story in a sermon, however, we ought not to stay at that level. If we do, we shall narrate the tale in a monotonous drone which will ruin its impressiveness. We need to modulate the pitch of our voices to match the undulating "emotional graph" of the illustration, thus bringing out its light and shade. "Vary the tone of your voice," Spurgeon advised his students. "Be like the weather. Have sun, sleet, rain, then dry up—anything but fog!"

For the finest effects the voice must be flexible, resilient, elastic. But how is it to become such? All voices are, of course, capable of stretching upward and downward to some degree. We have a natural speaking range of a few notes at least, but it can be extended in either direction by adopting certain simple measures. One of these is to go back to the piano and find our keynote once more. Having found it, we should speak raising the voice, semitone by semitone, sustaining and drawing out the words as we do, and see how high we can go without letting the tone get thin and shrill. After that we should try to go down the scale in the same manner, stopping in our descent before the voice becomes as deep and thick as the bark of a mastiff. Finally, we should try to discover the tone pattern of some familiar illustration, forming in our minds a sort of graph of the emotional rise and fall of the narrative, and reflect them in the variations of our voices. Such simple experiments, if persevered in, could widen the range of our vocal register, and increase our command of our organs of speech.

Another matter with which we shall have to reckon in relation to voice management is pace. Few things are more vital to the telling delivery of illustrations than tempo. Some set the pace far too slow. Of certain preachers it has been brutally said that "their words come out as if from the abdominal regions with the aid of a stomach-pump!" That is no tempo at which to tell a tale. Others set the pace much too fast. Surprisingly for a man of his type, Phillips Brooks came into this category. His delivery when preaching was alleged to be "rapid to the point of incoherency"; he once preached for a third of an hour at a rate of 227 words per minute! Such speedy speech is likely to cost the preacher and his congregation many an illustration. If, to quote Spurgeon's farcical figure, he tears along "like a wild horse with a hornet in its ear," some crucial detail may be missed for lack of which the whole illustration will become unintelligible. Somewhere between these two extremes lies the happy medium for the presentation of the word-picture. It must not be so slow that the people's interest is not kindled nor so swift that they cannot take it all in. "Say forth thy tale," counsels Chaucer, "and tarry not the time"—sound advice if taken in moderation.

Just as modulation of pitch is necessary to the effective presentation of illustrations, so is variation of pace. Different sorts of word-pictures require different rates of delivery. One would not relate a sad story at the same speed as one would a happy story. Besides, even within the single sermon-painting the pace of narration will need to fluctuate considerably if the illustration is to be feelingly conveyed. In a television interview, Rebecca West, the novelist, praised Harold Macmillan for his exceptional gifts as a raconteur. The aspect of the art of story-telling in which he especially excels, she stated, is his exquisite sense of timing. And that, she stressed, is the great thing in telling a story. It was a discerning judgment. Many fine illustrations, if not altogether wasted, have failed of their full effect because of faulty timing. To put our word-pictures movingly over we must vary the pace as well as the pitch.

A further matter claiming our notice in connection with voice management is volume. Arthur E. Gregory placed us all in his debt by reminding us that "a good sermon is not so much one that is well preached as one that is well heard." Here again ministers differ sharply. It does not take some long to reach "bawling point." They soon begin to bellow like bulls of Bashan and of them people say that although they have often heard better preachers, they have never heard preachers better! In getting illustrations across there is no necessity to emulate the Children of Israel surrounding the walls of Jericho. We do not need to shout except at points in the narrative where feelings run high. Certainly, we do not require, like some amateur organists, to have the "swells" out all the time. Never should our normal level of utterance be louder than is strictly essential to our being comfortably heard.

Analogous to this is the question of articulation. Some preachers suppose that it is vocal volume which makes them audible in the pulpit. In part, of course, it is. But no less imperative is clear and distinct enunciation. With reference to this the counsel commonly tendered is: "Look after the consonants and the vowels will look after themselves." On the whole, that is sage advice. Yet I would like to enter a couple of caveats. One is: "Watch that the vowels are not too broad and too long"; and the other, "Don't mouth the consonants overmuch in the manner of a donkey noisily munching hay." Anyhow we should beware of gabbled indistinctness.

On this subject of voice management only one matter more demands brief mention—the place and power of the pause in pulpit storytelling. Halting abruptly for a split second just before uttering some word or phrase we particularly want to stress in our story is a capital way of waking up the people to pay special attention to it. In preaching, the deliberate pause serves the same function as does the colon or dash in literature—it delivers the goods. And it is desirable to have the congregation on the alert when that happens. To be sure, certain preachers are given credit in this connection to which they are not entitled. There was, for example, the old Welsh divine of whom someone euphemistically said that "his pauses were mediums of pure oratory." What was meant was that the poor fellow stuttered! There was, too, the young Scots minister to whom the famous Thomas Chalmers listened and afterward remarked: "I like your sermon; you will make a good preacher: the pauses especially were magnificent." That was not intended as a left-handed compliment, and yet surely it was; praising a preacher for his pauses is rather like lauding a musician for his rests. It takes more than "magnificent pauses" to make either good musicians or good preachers. Nonetheless, in the putting over of illustrations, as well as elsewhere in the discourse, the pause does have its modest place. Only, we must not permit the pauses to be too long or too frequent lest we give our listeners the unpleasant impression that we are faint. Mental blackout, or what seems like it, in the preacher is hardly likely to prove illuminating to the hearers.

The second major matter connected with the actual putting across of our illustrations concerns gesture and things germane to it. And at this point we pass from the subject of speech to that of action.

Gesture is, of course, in some measure indigenous to us all. In moments of stress we use it without thinking, and when endeavoring to communicate with the deaf or with foreigners we find it of infinite assistance. It is a language of signs which everybody understands. And in preaching, what is it, after all, but the body trying to help the mind to express itself, the physical reflex of a supercharged imagination?

Imagination! There we touch the throbbing nerve of this business of narrative preaching. In our word-pictures we must visualize the scenes, persons, and situations if we would vitalize them. What a prominent feature imagination was in the ministries of the popular preachers of the past! As a conspicuous example, consider Alexander Whyte. Of him it was strikingly said that he was "full of eyes." His swift and apparently unpre-

207

meditated asides in the pulpit had a lightning-like power of instantaneous illumination. Speaking of Christ's crown of thorns, he suddenly broke out: "I wonder in what sluggard's garden they grew!" Picturing the man in the parable battering shamelessly at his neighbor's door at midnight, begging for bread, he exclaimed: "He comes back; he knocks again: 'Friend!' he cries, till the dogs bark at him!" Depicting the descent of the apostate angels, hurled over the battlements of heaven for their rebellion against the Most High, he applied his colors with something of the splendor and magnificence of Milton, and then all at once he interrupted himself to interject the shuddering whisper: "They are falling still!"

Needless to say, however, although gesture comes naturally to us all, it does not come equally to us all. Probably temperament has a good deal to do with it. Some preachers gesticulate much more than others. Sir James M. Barrie used to tell of a dynamic Scots minister, addicted to flinging his weight about in the pulpit, who dealt it with his fist such shattering blows that "the kirk had to have a standing contract with the carpenter to repair it once a month." Conversely, it astounds us to learn that Jonathan Edwards' terrific sermon on "Sinners in the Hands of an Angry God" was delivered quite impassively, the only motion of the preacher throughout being that of turning the pages of his manuscript.

Without imagination, and the gestures which spring from imagination, it would be practically impossible to put illustrations compellingly over.

Gestures are, of course, to be clearly distinguished from mannerisms. They are, in fact, as far apart as the poles. Gestures, at their best, are intentional, purposeful, significant, appropriate, illuminating; mannerisms are merely the irritating repetitions of meaningless muscular movements, a kind of clerical twitch. Where some preachers' gestures are concerned, the emphasis is definitely on the jest! In the pulpit they appear to adopt St. Vitus as their patron saint. They are "moving" preachers in the wrong sense, and the people soon grow weary of their crazy contortions. Of Friedrich W. Krummacher it is recorded that "his look and gesture were so expressive that deaf people followed the course of his preaching with intelligence." No deaf person would be likely to glean very much from the odd gesticulations in which some of us indulge. Far from thinking our gestures fit, they might be pardoned for supposing we were having a fit!

Is it not curious what trouble many of us have in the pulpit with our hands? John Cowan, taking his cue perhaps from the advertisements of a well-known firm, lists fifty-seven varieties of position in which they may be parked during preaching. Here are some of them: "In pockets, trousers, coat, vest, upper pocket, lower, rear; hung by thumb or immersed; hooked in vest arm-holes; clasped across tummy, ditto back; wadding handkerchief and unwadding; clenching lapels of coat; pounding desk; brushing hair; slapping at flies; full-arm, half-arm, finger; pointing at audience; twisting moustache; finger-tips together uplifted; fumbling with papers; pulling down vest; snapping; and, when not otherwise emphasizing the truth, sawing imaginary wood in the air." There is absolutely no need for all this. Deliberate, purposeful, expressive gestures can enable us, so to say, to get our hands off our hands. That in itself is no small gain.

It is not wise to gesticulate overmuch. When putting illustrations across, a larger amount of latitude is accorded the preacher than in the delivery of other parts of the discourse. But it is not advisable excessively to exploit this privilege. We should exercise a sane and balanced moderation and restraint and not use gesture any more than is strictly necessary for the purpose of impressive narration. While not becoming ponderous automatons, we should equally eschew gesticulatory gymnastics; and, while not standing stiffly in the pulpit with the stolid immobility of a tailor's dummy, neither should we turn ourselves into human windmills endlessly going through the same mechanical motions —in James Black's graphic phrase, "wagging our arms like a semaphore."

Gestures should, then, be appropriate, spontaneous, natural, restrained, dignified, and varied. Against such there is no law.

Perhaps at this point a word might usefully be interjected about what has been happily called "the holding power of the eye." One of the minister's finest assets in arresting and maintaining the attention of his hearers is the visual reciprocity which results from looking them squarely in the face while he speaks to them. Some preachers have the nervous habit of looking, while in the pulpit, all over the church as if they had lost something. Presently, they have—the interest of the congregation! "Preachers," comments John Bishop, "often forget the use of the eyes as an organ of speech." Pictorial preachers cannot afford to do so.

An extension of gesture is the acted illustration. Take three examples.

One is related of Samuel Chadwick. He had a powerful histrionic imagination and could be very dramatic in the delivery of his sermons. Preaching once on "Shew me a penny" (Luke 20:24), he produced such an effect by the manner in which he painted in the historic background of the text, actually living the incident over again before the people, that when in an imperious tone he called for the piece of money, one of the members of his congregation involuntarily slipped his hand into his trousers pocket and produced a coin.

Another is reported of F. Luke Wiseman. He likewise was adept at the acted illustration. Discoursing one day in Birmingham on the text, "If thy right hand offend thee, cut it off" (Matt. 5:30), he held out his right hand, gazed at it for awhile in silence, as if with shocked contempt, and then cried: "It struck the coward blow! It wrote the lying letter! It stole!" And thereupon, as he pretended to assume the role of executioner and to prepare to amputate his limb, a woman in the audience, overcome by the vividness of the dramatic representation, lost her self-control and exclaimed: "Nay, Mr. Wiseman, don't cut it off!"

The third acted illustration is taken from Paul E. Sangster's fascinating life of his father. The author writes: "The great Dr. Maltby was present when my father, in his Leeds days, went to Ilkley College and talked to the students about Moses slaying the Egyptian. As his excitement mounted he became Moses and looked this way and that and, on an impulse, struck the blow. Maltby, enraptured, forgot himself and shouted out: 'Oh, Sangster, do it again!' "

Such is the acted illustration at its best—a performance not wholly dissimilar from that of the stage, save that while, for the most part, the actor dramatizes fiction, the preacher dramatizes fact.

Not unlike acted illustrations are object illustrations. Only here, instead of simply seeking by illustrative physical movements to stimulate the fancy of our hearers, we actually show them the thing we are talking about. By using an object our aim is to keep the listeners' minds on the subject.

About the propriety of employing objects in preaching there is a sharp division of opinion. Some ministers advocate it and occasionally adopt it, others repudiate the idea with scorn. Doubtless it would be ill-advised to introduce too many sermons of that type into one's ministry. But, provided it is done rarely and restrainedly, I see no valid reason why an object should be objectionable.

Far more weighty than such considerations is the fact that the Bible itself furnishes not a few precedents for the practice. "Many," says Spurgeon, "condemn anything like the histrionic in preaching; I mean by that term the acting visibly, using signs and tokens which bring the truth to the eye as well as the ear. The prophets made use of that method very largely."

Indeed they did. Jeremiah wore a yoke, Ezekiel scrawled on a tile, Agabus seized Paul's girdle and bound him with it, and so on. Moreover the Master himself employed many objects to make plain his message—a penny, lilies, bread and wine, a towel, a cross. If Jesus illustrated in this way, who are we to say the method is inadmissible?

The following are two stories of modern preachers who dared to do it.

The first was enacted, if that is the proper word, in the new City Temple, London, not long before the retirement of Leslie Weatherhead. Here is an account of it:

It was a Harvest Thanksgiving Service. The front of the great building was gaily adorned with specimens of the fruits of the earth. Delighted with the display, the people feasted their eyes on it and doubtless dwelt with deep gratitude on the bounty of divine providence. At the close, however, they were shaken rather rudely out of their reverie by the ruthless realism of the preacher's remark. "You have been gazing at the display of food for an hour," he told them, "and during that hour one thousand people died of starvation in the Far East."

The object lesson—if the old lady in the story wouldn't have minded my calling her an "object"—is equally unconventional and unforgettable. W. E. Sangster, who devised it, wrote of it as follows:

Years ago, I ran a beauty competition in the church of which I was then minister. There had been an epidemic of beauty competitions. You couldn't open the newspaper without reading about them. The town council, the cinemas, the trade councils, this interest and that interest, were all running beauty competitions. So I ran one at my church. Only, my beauty competition was unlike any other of which I had heard. It was a beauty competition for people over seventy. I will not deny that it caused a tremendous amount of interest in the town and, when the awards had been made, the portrait of the winning lady appeared in most of the London dailies. Some folk thought it was rather odd of me. I regarded it as one of the most sensible things I ever did. I had a purpose in it—an inwardness which the discerning recognized. The old lady who won—and who only took part by my great persuasion—was a saint. Her face shone with a glory which was not of earth. One of the reporters, I remember, said to me: "Strange idea, sir, this beauty competition of yours. I reckon I'm a bit of a judge of these things—and indeed on my paper it is my speciality. I am always attending beauty competitions, and I have seen scores of prize-winners, but there is something about that old lady that is different." He saw it, though he could not understand it. I have sometimes wondered whether the comment I made to him was really enlightening. I said: "Well, you see, her face is made, and the ones that you normally study are only made-up!" [2]

Once more, despite Dr. Sangster's suspicion of the reporter's incomprehension, who can doubt that the point of that object illustration got over to thousands who would never otherwise have thought of such a thing? The French have a proverb to the effect that sin makes one ugly. How better could one illustrate the contrary—that holiness makes beautiful—than by the somewhat daring experiment of Dr. Sangster?

At this juncture we may spare a moment or two in which to bestow a fleeting glance on a rare and highly specialized type of action-picture—the musical illustration. F. Luke Wiseman was in the habit of using it on occasion. "Many a time," writes Harold Murray, "I have known him in the middle of a rousing speech at an anniversary meeting, cross the platform to a piano and electrify the audience with an unexpected song illustration." Most of us are not versatile or unselfconscious enough to attempt anything of that sort with success. The best we can do in the circumstances is to enlist the musical aid of others in illustration of our theme. A good soloist can do it superbly, or a duet, a trio, a quartet, or a whole choir, and the illuminative sound-picture can either precede or follow the sermon.

John Grimshaw supplies from his own ministerial memories a graphic and impressive instance. "I shall not soon forget an incident in my own ministry," he records; "I had been preaching on the words, '[They] took up the body, and buried it, and

[2] Paul E. Sangster, Dr. Sangster (London: Epworth Press, 1962), p. 78.

213

went and told Jesus' (Matt. 14:12). At the close, a member of the choir, with a rich alto voice, sang:

> Go bury thy sorrow,
> The world hath its share
> Go bury it deeply,
> Go hide it with care;
> Go think of it calmly,
> When curtained by night:
> Go tell it to Jesus
> And all will be right.

The effect was electric."

And now, to close, let us note that in getting an illustration across it is crucially important to know just when to put on the brake. More than once in these pages we have reminded ourselves that in delivery the length of the word-picture must be adjusted at the preacher's discretion to the exigencies of the situation. Sometimes that will mean devoting to its presentation what might seem an inordinate amount of precious time. But if the illustration is first-rate the time will not be wasted. Lionel Fletcher, an accomplished exponent of the sermon-illustrator's art, once gave this advice to A. Lindsay Glegg: "Don't hurry the telling of your illustrations. Tell them well. Build up the background, picture the whole scene, and make it live before the eyes of the congregation. I will take ten valuable minutes, if necessary, to tell a story."

Such expansiveness, however, must not be allowed to become excessive. We may give the horse a free rein, but we must not let him run away with us; and we must ever be on the alert against the perils of improvisation. Always we must keep a sharp lookout for an effective place at which to stop, and when we find it we must not ignore the traffic signal. Many illustrations lose vastly in impressiveness because the preacher fails to recognize the halt sign. We ought not to go ambling on and rambling on after we have reached our goal. A counsel I had better apply here!

There is a lovely story—told, I believe, of Leonardo da Vinci—that once in his studio he started work on a large canvas. For a while he labored at it—choosing the subject, planning the perspective, sketching the outline, applying the colors, with his own inimitable genius. Then suddenly he ceased—the painting still unfinished—and, summoning one of his students, bade him carry on with the work. The student protested that he was alike unworthy and unable to complete the great painting which his master had commenced. But da Vinci silenced him. "Will not what I have done inspire you to do your best?" he inquired.

Just so with Jesus and ourselves. Our divine Master began two thousand years ago—by what he was, by what he said, by what he did, and supremely by what he suffered—to illustrate his message, and he has left us to finish the picture. It is a task from which we may well shrink; and yet, as we address ourselves to it, we shall find in it not only challenge but inspiration.

Index of Authors Quoted